INDIAN BALLADS

INDIAN BALLADS,

AND OTHER POEMS.

WILLIAM WATERFIELD

GYAN

Published by

GYAN

Gyan Publishing House
5, Ansari Road
Daryaganj, New Delhi-110002
Phone: 011-47034999, 9811692060
E-mail: books@gyanbooks.com

Distribution Network
gyanbooks.com
India, USA, Canada, UK, Australia, France

ISBN: 978-81-212-8680-0 (PB)
First Published, 1868

2nd Impression 2023

Printed at: Gyan Press, Delhi.

INDIAN BALLADS
Author: William Waterfield

INDIAN BALLADS,

AND OTHER POEMS.

BY

WILLIAM WATERFIELD.

LONDON: SMITH, ELDER AND CO
1868.

CONTENTS.

INDIAN BALLADS.

MISCELLANEOUS BALLADS.

ALBUM VERSES.

ALBUM VERSES—*continued.*

Dedication.

WHAT gallant ship that sailed for summer skies,
  And twice would cross the misty-slumbrous Line,
Was richlier freighted with her merchandise,
  Than we who carried love and prayers of thine?
  What bring we back? Ores from a golden mine.
Where Love Who left the joy that never dies,
To save a world and gladden weary eyes,
  Through dross of mortal passion still will shine?
Or pearls of human faith and constancy,
  Prahlāda's firmness—Sītā ever true—
And the sweet love of plighted Rukminī?
  And be the venture great, the profits few,
  Thou wilt not reckon harshly for thy due,
Nor slight the poor return we render thee.

INDIAN BALLADS.

INDIAN BALLADS,

ETC. ETC.

Hymn to Ushas (Aurora).

(FROM THE "RIG VEDA.")

[The hymns of the Vedas are addressed chiefly to natural objects. An attempt has been made, while giving some of the most poetical ideas, to retain the simplicity of style and irregularity of metre.]

1.

USHAS I praise
Of the brilliant rays,
Who hath dwelt in heaven of old.
The gates of the sky,
As the sun draws nigh,
Her lovely hands unfold.

2.

Goddess of Morn,
Heavenly-born,
Many-tinted, enrobed in white,
A hundred cars
Dost thou lead to the wars
Thou wagest for us 'gainst the bands of Night.

3.

Thou leadest the crowd,
Like a warrior proud,
Whose march is in the van;
For the realms of Night,
With thy weapons of light,
Thou art conquering back for man.

4.

From afar, from afar,
Dost thou harness thy car,
Beyond the bright sunrise;
As thy course proceeds
On thy purple steeds,
Thou gladdenest mortal eyes.

5.

To the golden-eyed[1]
Thou com'st as a bride
Whom her mother's hands adorn :
The demons of Night,
Who would mar our rite,
Are chased by the breath of Morn.

6.

Glad cries are heard
From beast and bird,
The bounteous goddess knowing ;
With truthful voice
Doth each rejoice
To greet the All-bestowing.

7.

For wealth or fame,
Or a holy name,
The sons of men are striving ;
Their slumber they break
When thou dost wake,
At thy silent call reviving.

8.

Thou old, yet ever young!
Unchanged all change among!
Thy journeyings who may number?
As a matron wise and fair
Intent on housewife care,
Thou rousest thy sons from slumber.

9.

Call the labourers from rest;
Call the birds from out their nest;
Call the priest to the hall of praise:
But let the niggard sleep
In the dark unlovely deep,
Afar from thy lightning rays.

10.

They all are past and gone
On whom thou erst hast shone,
And thou shalt shine on those who see not yet the light;
But ours the present day;
Then, ere it roll away,
The favour of the gods let us with prayers invite.

Hymn to Indra.

Indra is the Jupiter of the Hindūs, the representation of the visible firmament. He is therefore attended by the forty-nine winds. (It was prophesied to Indra that Marut, the wind, would be too powerful for his control. He therefore struck him with his thunderbolt, dividing him into seven fragments, and again, crosswise, each of these into seven. Thus the whole are never united, but counteract each other.)

He is also lord of the rainbow and the thunderbolt, and of the thousand eyes or stars, though a later legend has been invented to explain this title.

He is, again, like Jupiter, leader of the gods in their wars with the Titans; and one of his most common names is the "Render of Cities." Māyā, or illusion, is among the strongest weapons in the superhuman armoury of the Hindūs.

He is, lastly, King of Swarga, the temporary Paradise of the good, with its immortal city, Amarāvatī, and its five celestial trees.

But, to do the Hindūs justice, and show how superior their creed is, *in scheme*, to that of Greece and Rome, it must be explained that no hymns later than the Vedas would be addressed to Indra, or any but the Supreme Deity, either in one of the persons of the Triad, or in an incarnation or energy (imaged as the consort) of one of the latter. Nor would they look, as the object of their hopes, to Swarga, which, after a period of enjoyment to the senses proportioned to merit, leads to other births in an earthly state. The only reward considered worth obtaining is union with the Supreme Spirit, and emancipation from the troubles and temptations of a mortal existence.]

1.

God of the varied bow!
  God of the thousand eyes!
From all the winds that blow
  Thy praises rise;
Forth through the world they go,
Hymning to all below
Thee, whom the blest shall know,
  Lord of the skies!

2.

Rending the guilty town,
  Leading celestial hosts,
Hurling the demons down
  To the drear coasts:
Still with thy lightning frown
Winning thee wide renown,
Till the wild waters drown
  All their proud boasts.

3.

Whom thy dread weapon finds,
  Striking the mark afar,
Them thy just anger binds
  In the fierce war:

Rebels! their frenzied minds
Thus thine illusion blinds,—
Seven times seven winds
  Wafting thy car.

4.

So, by the fivefold tree,
  Where the bright waters run,
We, who impurity
  Heedfully shun,
In Amarāvatī,
Indra, shall dwell with thee,
From earth's pollution free,
  When life is done.

5.

God by the gods obeyed,
  Hear thou our feeble cry!
Lend us thy sovereign aid,
  Lord of the sky!
Of our fierce foes afraid,
Fainting, distressed, dismayed,
To thy protecting shade
  Hither we fly.

The Sacrifice of Daksha.

[This is a favourite subject of Hindū sculpture, especially on the temples of Shiva, such as the caves of Elephanta and Ellora. It, no doubt, is an allegory of the contest between the followers of Shiva and the worshippers of the Elements, who observed the old ritual of the Vedas, in which the name of Shiva is never mentioned.]

DAKSHA for devotion
Made a mighty feast;
Milk and curds and butter,
Flesh of bird and beast,

Rice and spice and honey,
Sweetmeats, ghī and gur,[2]
Gifts for all the Brāhmans,
Food for all the poor.

At the gates of Gangā[3]
Daksha held his feast;
Called the gods unto it,
Greatest as the least.

All the gods were gathered
  Round with one accord;
All the gods but Umā,[4]
  All but Umā's lord.

Umā sat with Shiva
  On Kailāsa[5] hill;
Round them stood the Rudras[6]
  Watching for their will.

Who is this that cometh,
  Lilting to his lute?
All the birds of heaven
  Heard his music, mute.

Round his head a garland
  Rich of hue was wreathed;
Every sweetest odour
  From its blossoms breathed.

'Tis the Muni[7] Nārad;
  'Mong the gods he fares,
Ever making mischief
  By the tales he bears.

"Hail to lovely Umā!
Hail to Umā's lord!
Wherefore are they absent
From her father's board?

"Multiplied his merits
Would be truly thrice,
Could he gain your favour
For his sacrifice."

Wroth of heart was Umā;
To her lord she spake:—
"Why dost thou, the mighty,
Of no rite partake?

"Straight I speed to Daksha
Such a sight to see:
If he be my father,
He must welcome thee."

Wondrous was in glory
Daksha's holy rite;
Never had creation
Viewed so brave a sight.

Gods, and nymphs, and fathers,
Sages, Brāhmans, sprites,—
Every diverse creature
Wrought that rite of rites.

Quickly then a quaking
Fell on all from far;
Umā stood amidst them
On her lion car.

"Greeting, gods and sages,
Greeting, father mine!
Work hath wondrous virtue,
Where such aids combine.

"Guest-hall never gathered
Goodlier company:
Seemeth all are welcome,—
All the gods but me."

Spake the Muni Daksha,
Stern and cold his tone:—
"Welcome thou, too, daughter,
Since thou com'st alone.

"But thy frenzied husband[8]
Suits another shrine;
He is no partaker
Of this feast of mine.

"He who walks the darkness
Loves no deeds of light;
He who herds with demons
Shuns each kindly sprite.

"Let him wander naked,—
Wizard weapons wield,—
Dance his frantic measure
Round the funeral field.

"Art thou yet delighted
With the reeking hide,
Body smeared with ashes,
Skulls in necklace tied?

"Thou to love this monster!
Thou to plead his part!
Know the moon and Gangā
Share that faithless heart.

"Vainly art thou vying
With thy rivals' charms:
Are not coils of serpents
Softer than thine arms?"

Words like these from Daksha
Daksha's daughter heard;
Then a sudden passion
All her bosom stirred:

Eyes with fury flashing,
Speechless in her ire,
Headlong did she hurl her
'Mid the holy fire.

Then a trembling terror
Overcame each one,
And their minds were troubled
Like a darkened sun;

And a cruel Vision,
Face of lurid flame,
Umā's Wrath Incarnate,
From the altar came.

Fiendlike forms by thousands
  Started from his side;
'Gainst the sacrificers
  All their might they plied:

Till the saints availed not
  Strength like theirs to stay,
And the gods distracted
  Turned and fled away.

Hushed were hymns and chanting;
  Priests were mocked and spurned;
Food defiled and scattered;
  Altars overturned.—

Then, to save the object
  Sought at such a price,
Like a deer in semblance
  Sped the sacrifice.

Soaring toward the heavens,
  Through the sky it fled;
But the Rudras chasing
  Smote away its head.

Prostrate on the pavement
Daksha fell dismayed :—
"Mightiest, thou hast conquered ;
Thee we ask for aid.

"Let not our oblations
All be rendered vain ;
Let our toilsome labour
Full fruition gain."

Bright the broken altars
Shone with Shiva's form ;
"Be it so !" His blessing
Soothed that frantic storm.

Soon his anger ceases,
Though it soon arise ;—
But the Deer's Head[9] ever
Blazes in the skies.

The Song of the Koïl.[10]

O youths and maidens, rise and sing!
The Koïl is come who leads the spring:
The buds that were sleeping his voice have heard,
And the tale is borne on by each nesting bird.

The trees of the forest have all been told;
They have donned their mantles of scarlet and gold; [11]
To welcome him back they are bravely dressed,
But he loves the blossoming mango best.

The Koïl is come, glad news to bring!
On the blossoming mango he rests his wing;
Though its hues may be dull, it is sweet, oh! sweet,
And its shade and its fruit the wanderer greet.

The Koïl is come, and the forests ring:
He has called aloud to awake the Spring,—
Spring the balmy, the friend of Love,
The bodiless god who reigns above.[12]

Oh! sad were the hearts of the gods that day
When the worlds all mourned the oppressor's sway;
When the oracle promised deliverance none
Till Shiva the wrathful should lend his son.[13]

But Shiva the wrathful he recked not of that
Where on Himavān's[14] side as a hermit he sat:
And there was not a dweller on Meru[15] would dare
To break his devotion, and show him their prayer.

Yet not even the frown of Destruction could awe
The loveliest form that Creation e'er saw;
Eternal in youth, he thought it foul shame
That the Eldest of Beings dishonoured his name.

He hath mounted his parrot that flashed in the sun;
He hath pointed with blossoms his arrows each one:[16]
Of the sweet, sweet cane he hath shapen his bow;
And his string is of bees in a long black row.

Soon Kāma is come to the Being he sought;
His visage was haggard with watching and thought;
His body was lean, and his limbs were shrunk;
His colour was wan, and his eyes were sunk.

His thick black locks in a knot were tied ;
His loins were wrapped with a tiger's hide ;
His skin with ashes was smeared and grey ;
And spread beneath him a deer-skin lay.

He moved not, nor spoke, save in telling his beads
On the rosary strung of the jungle seeds ; [17]
Yet his head was awful, a god's to view,
And gemmed with the moon and the Ganges' dew.

And little did Shiva the wrathful care
For the flag which flaunted so bravely there ;
Though the fish [18] was flashing with jewels and gold,
He moved not his eyes, and his beads he told.

But archly does young-eyed Kāma smile
On those who would foil him by force or by guile ;
And his keenest shaft to the string he laid,
As he called to that presence the mountain-maid. [19]

The love-shaft flew from the bow-string fast,
As the child of the snows in her beauty passed ;
And the cream-white lotus [20] blushed rosy red
Where the blood of the god from his wound was shed.

Oh! sharp is the arrowy blossom's smart,
For the mango flower ne'er missed the heart;
And the work of the gods is fairly done,
And help shall arise out of Shiva's son.[21]

But woe for that image of loveliness, woe!
Which the worlds of creation no longer shall know;
In Shiva's first wrath at the breach of his vow,
Consumed by the flame-darting eye of his brow.[22]

But the flames could not weaken Immortal Might;
He is born in the heart[23] in the spring-time bright.
Whose is the breast where the god shall dwell?
O youths and maidens, you can tell.

The Churning of the Ocean.

SAD and bitter was the season,
  In the lonely days of yore,
When the mighty demon's treason
  Vexed the world from shore to shore :

When the Suras[24] were but mortal,
  And they fell by force or guile :
While the Asurs[25] to Heaven's portal
  Near and nearer drew the while.

Came the gods by Brahmā bidden—
  Doubt and dread in every face ;
Long they held a council hidden—
  Strait and evil seemed their case.

Vishnu prayed they then to save them :
  Only him their trust they made :
Deep the counsel which he gave them,
  When they looked to him for aid.

When they left the realms of pleasure,
  "Know ye not, Asuras wise,"
Thus they said, "the priceless treasure
  Ocean hideth from our eyes?

"Sweet is life the while one liveth,
  But death cometh soon or late;
Win with us the draught which giveth
  Life exempt from change of fate.

"If to churning of the ocean
  Our united strength we bring,
From the swift and swirling motion
  Will that virtuous liquor spring."

Then they made a pact between them,
  Gods and demons in that tide;
Joyously did they demean them
  As they laboured side by side.

Mandar first, that mighty mountain,
  From his roots they wrenched and tore;
Him with tree and rock and fountain
  For their churning-staff they bore.

Shesha[26] next, the hundred-headed,
World-support—the Serpent King—
Round the mountain him, the dreaded,
Wound they for their churning string.

Still their work remained unready;
For their staff support they lack,
Till by Vishnu's grace 'twas steady
On the eternal Tortoise'[27] back.

But the demons, danger scorning,
Heedless seized the poison head,
While the gods at Vishnu's warning
Safely grasped the tail instead.

So they ranged their ranks asunder;
So they toiled with might and glee:
When was ever heard a wonder
Like the churning of the sea!

Eager strove they, struggling, straining;
Round the mountain whirled and swung;
Shesha writhed, the task disdaining;
High their crests the billows flung.

White the width of waters boiling
  Roared and burst around the hill:
Ocean, all the labour foiling,
  Battled for his treasures still.

Lo! at last the waves are breaking!
  Lo! a prize of marvel won!
From his manes the foam-drops shaking,
  Sea-green courser of the sun.[28]

Lo! Airāvat's[29] form stupendous!
  'Tis the beast that Indra rides,
Spouting from his trunk tremendous
  Fountains o'er his monstrous sides.

Cow of plenty,[30] boon-bestowing,
  Yieldeth now the rifled sea:
Now with sweetest blossoms blowing
  Swarga's[31] first and fairest tree.

Eager strove they, struggling, straining:
  Round and round the mountain swung;
Shesha gasped, the toil sustaining;
  Loud the thundering echoes rung;

Whirled the waste of waters raging:
  White and wide the yeasty froth;
Ocean fiercer warfare waging
  Held his treasures still in wrath.

Forms of brightness, silvern, golden,
  Moon and Sun by turn appear:
They by Soma, Sūrya, holden,
  Rule the changes of the year.

Vishnu gained his lustrous jewel,
  Conch and disc [32] instinct with life;
Shiva won that weapon [33] cruel
  None but he can bend in strife.

Shadowy shapes of perfect beauty [34]
  Form amidst the creaming foam;
Nymphs who—meed of warrior's duty—
  Make the Swarga bowers their home.

Eager strove they, struggling, straining;
  Round the mountain whirled and swung;
Shesha panted, uncomplaining;
  Flames from rocks and bushes sprung;

Billows raging, roaring, raving;
  Stirred the waters' utmost deep;
Ocean's foamy banners waving
  Still their choicest treasures keep.

Dhanwantari,[35] sage physician,
  Next his priceless casket brings—
Healing hand, if ill condition
  E'er might touch celestial things.

Now a vision comes enthralling—
  Lakshmī comes, the queen of grace;[36]
Gods and demons prostrate falling
  Bow before that lovely face.

By the charmer unaffected
  Sur or Asur stood not one;
Thus by rival hands neglected
  All their toil was nigh undone.

Slow, more slow, was Mandar turning:
  Calmer grew the angry main:
Ocean from the fearful churning
  Deemed the prize his own again.

But the demons fainter growing
  Could not win so fair a bride;
She, herself her hand bestowing,
  Seated her at Vishnu's side.

Eager strained they, struggling, striving;
  Round and round Mount Mandar swung:
Shesha, drooping, scarce surviving,—
  On his jaws the poison hung.

Nigh those jaws of horror gaping
  All the demons faint and tire,
Till beyond control escaping
  Burst around the stream of fire.

Then had earth and sky been blasted,
  Then the seven oceans blazed,
Had the flaming torrent lasted—
  While the gods in stupor gazed—

But that Shiva, strong in aiding,
  Drained himself the fatal draught:
While the throat-stain [87] never fading
  Shows how fierce a cup he quaffed.

Lo, once more a sight surprising!
  Lo, two maidens side by side!
Each amid the waters rising
  Bears a beaker from the tide.

Roaring sink the seas defeated:
  Rests the serpent: stands the hill:
All their labour now completed,
  Let the toilers take their fill.

Then the Asuras dazed and hasting
  Seized the larger, fairer flask;
While the gods the Amrit[38] tasting
  Gained the profit of the task.

Yet each eager demon seeker
  Boasted loud—"the prize is mine;"[39]
For from that deceitful beaker
  First was poured the enchanter, Wine.

Only of the Amrit flagon
  One more wary tasted too,—
Rāhu—spite his shape of dragon—
  Mingled with the Sura crew.

Sūrya soon the craft espying,
  Vishnu cleft his form in twain:
But the head[40] lives on undying—
  Mortal yet the fish-like train.

Sun and moon his hate pursuing
  Chases ever night and day:
Woe for earth's and man's undoing,
  Should he seize them on their way!

The Fourth Avatāra.

1.

SING we to him who reigneth on high,
The first of the sacred three:[41]
In the world beneath, and the earth, and sky.
As far as the golden walls[42] extend
Where light must vanish and life must end,
Is none so great as he.

2.

Sing we to him whose couch is borne
By the many-headed snake:[43]
By elemental discord torn,
Nature her rest must take,
'Midst the world of waters wide
Tossing round on every side,

Till the god his slumbers break,
When the destined hour is nigh,
And bid a new creation wake
To life and energy.

3.

All-preserving, all-creating,
All-destroying he ;[44]
From his essence generating
All things that e'er shall be.
Nought is done
Beneath the sun,
Within the golden wall,
But he, before the worlds begun,
Hath predetermined all.

4.

Still the work he loveth best
Is to give the weary rest ;
To remove, in mortal birth,
The burdens of the groaning earth ;
And with resistless arm to free

His followers who, in good or ill,
Shall hold their faith unshaken still,
Few and feeble though they be;
For those who look to him for aid
Nought on earth shall make afraid.

5.

'Twas thus he humbled Bali's pride,[45]
Spanning the skies at a single stride:
And to earth the Vedas gave,
Hidden long in ocean-cave,
Till the conflict dire was ended:
And, the holy king to save,
From out the all-destroying wave
His radiant horn extended.

6.

Sing we the deeds of the Rāmas three,[46]
With ploughshare, axe, and bow:
Of him in vest of blue arrayed,
The wielder of the awful blade,
The spouse of Revatī:
Of him who cleft the house of snow,

Where, through the deep and winding length,
  The sacred waters flow
Of Gangā rushing in her strength
  Upon the world below;
Who, in his righteous ire,
  Unnumbered hosts o'erthrew,
And, to avenge his slaughtered sire,
  The haughty tyrants slew:
Or last, of him, Ayodhyā's boast,
  Who bridged the roaring deep:
Who quelled the demon host,
  Though their arms were mighty, their walls
    were steep,
And on the barbarous coast
  Undying fame did reap.

7.

  By his side
  His radiant bride,
Lovely Sītā,[47] lotus-eyed;
  From the giant's fierce embrace,—
Sorely tempted, sorely tried,—
  Rescued by the monkey race;

Ever constant, ever true,
  From the sea of milk descending,
Each various incarnation through,
  His glorious steps attending.

8.

Most precious of all treasures she [18]
That rose from out the teeming sea,
When the gods and demons strove
  The cup of life to gain;
    From every land
    The heavenly band
  Of watchers thronged her hand to obtain;
Yet, well discerning Vishnu's love,
  She went with him to reign.

9.

But, when misfortune on her cast
  Suspicion and evil blame,
The ordeal strange she passed
  To clear her injured name;
High-hearted in her purity,
  She dared the raging flame;

Like the wind that blows
From the mount of snows
The holy fire became,
And, from their self-moving cars on high,[49]
The heavenly powers
Rained down flowers,
And sang her spotless fame.

10.

Yet best we love to sing
The universal King,[50]
When, for his faithful servants' good,
Beneath the tyrant's sway oppressed,
Clad in his yellow vest,
The god in lowly guise
A simple herd-boy stood,
In Vrindā's holy wood;—
O chief of mysteries,
Hard to be understood!

11.

His lotus eyes
Our hearts surprise
From his face of the cloud-dark hue; [51]

As the stars shine bright
Through the purple night,
Or the sea-fire flashes its living light
From the ocean's depths of blue.

12.

But a fiercer form he bore
In the evil days of yore,
When every region groaned beneath a tyrant's sway;
When every living thing
The golden-mailèd [52] king
Acknowledged as supreme to worship and obey.

13.

So great the penance done,
By Diti's [53] mighty son,
A wondrous gift he won
From the Creator's hand:
O'er earth he ruled, and sea, and skies,
And made the trembling deities
Within his palace walls in menial garb to stand.
None might strive with him in fight
Beneath the eye of day;
None beneath the clouds of night
Might the wicked Rājā slay;

He no hostile form need doubt
In earth, or sky, or sea;
Within his palace and without,
From death or danger free;
Man, and beast, and form divine
Vainly should 'gainst him combine.

14.

But with such power entrusted he
Waxed wanton in his pride;
And with a frantic jealousy
The friends of Vishnu eyed.

15.

Where shall be found, oh! where,
One faithful earnest heart,
Unblenchingly to dare
The torture's fiery smart,
And raise a suppliant prayer
Before the eternal throne?
O fools! by worldly threatenings cowed,
Before a mortal's feet they bowed,
And rendered him the worship proud
They owed to one alone.

The Brāhmans misinterpreted
  What truths the Vedas taught:
The people, by their priests misled,
  No real wisdom sought:
The Scriptures were no longer read:
  None made the ablutions due;
The expectant manes were not fed;
  The poor no helper knew;
The Gurus[54] were dishonourèd;
  The holy kine were slain;
For far and wide doth evil spread
  Beneath an evil reign.

16.

On those who slight the god's command,
  What vengeance shall he do?
Shall floods destroy the impious land,
  And whelm the world anew?
Or shall the clouds of thunder, big with woes,
That bring the iron age's fearful close,
  Amidst the affrighted skies
  Before their time arise?
Or shall the obedient trees again
Hear their Creator's word, as when

His mandate bade them sweep
O'er hill and desert, rock and fen,
With rapid growth unchecked, till men
Were forced into the deep?[55]
The breezes had no power to blow,
And all that fearful shade below
Was silent as the tomb:
The restless sands did forests know,
And Himavān[56] his crest of snow
Veiled with a verdant plume;
So close the countless trunks were set,
And interlacing branches met,
The earth with rain was never wet,
No ray dispelled the gloom;
Till from their vigil in the seas
The saints[57] arising reached the bank,
And, where they passed, the conscious trees
Before their awful presence shrank.

17.

The lord of mercy deemeth not
All evil and unsound,
If still one unpolluted spot,
Unscathed by sin, be found.

He sees, amongst the Rājā's train,
One incorrupt of heart remain
  Amidst the tempters round.
Before Hiranyakashipu [58]
Though princes bow and sages sue,—
  Though all the earth adore,—
Unmoved by worldly pomp, his eye,
Endued with wisdom from on high,
To Vishnu's throne beyond the sky
  Hath learned in faith to soar.

18.

The monarch's son, Prahlāda styled,
Of guilty sire the guiltless child,—
  Him no temptations could o'erwhelm,
    Still faithful found when tried,—
  The heir to all his father's realm,
    But not his father's pride.

19.

The pleasures of a royal state
  Have made e'en sages fall;
The threatenings of the earthly great
Cause saints from right to deviate;

He knew how vain our mortal fate,
  And overcame them all.
His sire none more obedient knew,
Yet served he not beyond the due
  Of fathers and of kings;
His heart was set on wisdom true,
  From Vishnu's self that springs.

20.

"Son," said the king, "no longer praise
Those puny gods of other days,
  Whose power has passed away;
A mightier sceptre than the old
(Which thou thyself perchance may'st hold)
  Do all the worlds obey.
Or, if they still some reverence claim,
Through Shiva, not through Vishnu's name,
  Thy vows will most avail;
He was a mighty prince indeed;
His acts of vengeance we may read
  In many an ancient tale.
But, on his distant lotus-seat
  Enthronèd with his bride,
Lies Vishnu in oblivion sweet,

Nor heeds the world beside.
If thou wouldst praise him, thither go ;
For not within these realms below
Shall he, our race's deadliest foe,
By thee be glorified!"

21.

To him Prahlāda answer made :—
"Father, in all things be obeyed
(As best beseems) thy will ;
But, when my eyes behold the land,
And view the workings of his hand,
How can my tongue be still ?
And how can I associate
With Shiva's sullen train,
Who weave before his temple-gate,
Their frantic dance, or meditate
Within the awful fane ?

22.

"It was not from the will of their master's might
That the earth in its loveliness golden bright,
And the changeful weft of the day and night,
And the heavens whose glories are infinite,

Into young creation burst:
He loveth the blood of the mystic rite,
And he smileth on men as they rush to fight,
Like demons for gore athirst:
In the funeral field, with fiend and sprite,
He worketh his orgies dire,
As they dance around by the spectral light
Of the slowly-fading pyre.
When the fight is done,
'Neath the setting sun,
He hastes with his horrid train:
He quaffs the blood,
In a ghastly flood
As it lies on the battle-plain;
And he loves to bedeck
With skulls his neck,
As he strides o'er the heaps of slain.

23.

"But Vishnu seeks to bless
The earth with happiness,
As in his yellow dress
He roams the woodland shades;

'Tis there he spends the sunny hours :
Leader of Heaven's benignant powers,
He haunts the groves and forest bowers,—
His necklace, of the forest flowers,—
  His train, the forest maids.
Kind to the poor, and mercy's lord ;
How well such names accord
  With true devotion, the preserver's claim !
No penance fraught with fear,
To gloomy Shiva dear,
Shall have such power above
As pure and earnest love,
  And faith on Hari's[59] name.
Thus Vishnu doth fulfil
To each his separate will
  Of honour, wealth, or fame ;
But if, puffed up by power and pride,
From truth and right they start aside,
Compassionate, not even then
His mercy fails the sons of men :
Before misfortune's chilling blast
Down from their dizzy greatness cast.
  They turn to him again.

24.

Yet he those paths of danger never knows,
On whom the god his chiefest favour shows;
Who gives no boon
Decaying soon,
But saves from lasting woes,
And union with himself through future time bestows.

25.

"For countless wealth, or magic might,
Or wondrous charms, or strength in fight,
Or universal reign,
To Mahādeva[60] be thy suit;
All worldly blessings as its fruit
Thy penance shall attain.
But they who Vishnu serve,
Nor from his precepts swerve,
Though poverty the lot they must endure on earth,
Among the spirits blest,
Dwell in untroubled rest,
Absorbed in his divinity, exempt from future birth."

26.

Scarce the concluding word
The king of giants heard,
And marked Prahlāda's faith, by menace undeterred;
"Chiefs of my host," he cried, "obey,
And with the traitorous wretch away,
Who dares acknowledge in my realm a rival to my sway."

27.

Straight at their monarch's call
Attendant in the hall,
Appeared the demon chiefs, of mighty stature all.
Prahlāda shrank not, but his eye
Unquailing raised he to the sky,
As though he said,—
"By Vishnu's aid
Your warriors I defy."

28.

"Strike!" cried the monarch; but in vain
The weapons fall, and fall again:

They swerve aside, nor reach his steadfast breast :
  As rowers, when with sinewy strain
  They strive some sheltering isle to gain,—
  Hurled by the eddies to the roaring main,
In mute despair the weary oarsmen rest.

29.

"Away with these!" the angry Rājā cries,
"The fire a surer punishment supplies."
Then forth the unresisting prince they drew :
An unseen power the flames obedient knew,
    And parted wide
    On either side,
  And wreathed their waving coils around,
    As though an arch of triumph they supplied,
  And his most holy head with glory crowned.

30.

  The tiger slunk away
  Before the intended prey :
Unharmed, in faith did he the cup envenomed
    drink :
Hurled from the mountain precipice's brink,

As soft he sank to rest,
On the earth's rocky breast,
As the descending lark doth sink,
Her hymn of thanks complete, upon her nest.

31.

The learned Brāhmans came,
Before the sacred flame
They wrought their sorceries dread :
The spirit feared to face
The shield of Vishnu's grace,
And shrieking smote the sorcerers in his stead.

32.

Thereat a voice was heard so soft and clear.
It thrilled the heart with love and fear :
" Well hast thou done ;
Thy prayer, whate'er it be, I hear,
Ask thou a boon, my son."
Prahlāda due obeisance made,
And thus with reverent voice he said :—
" If such be in thy will,
Though those their lofty birth abuse,
The works of righteousness refuse.

And seek thy saints to kill;
Yet in thy mercy-loving breast
Short time do wrath and anger rest;
Think, they are Brāhmans still:
Upon them look with pitying eye:
Forgiven, they from sin may fly,
And leave the paths of ill."

33.

Up rose the Brāhmans then,
And they spake before the king:
"Ours is the strength of men,
And their aid thy demons bring.
But with thy holy son
In vain would we contend;
For his righteousness hath won
The Eternal for his friend.
Him, Rājā, do not thou forget;
Though long his anger sleep,
Rebellious princes never yet
Destruction failed to reap.
His shafts of vengeance are not spent,
Though mercy bids them wait:
Unless thou dost in time repent,
Thou shalt—when all too late."

34.

" Then let him live, since live he must.
Till he shall loathe to live ;
Till all the joy of living rust,
Craving, from him he made his trust.
The death he cannot give.
Bear him, ye demons, far away ;
Beneath the ocean's utmost deep,
Where never reached the light of day,
Let him and all his treasons sleep.
With mountains piled above his head,
Sunk in the water's oozy bed,
Unseen and unrememberèd,
How can his doctrines further spread ? "

35.

There many a day
Prahlāda lay,
While rocks above him tower ;
Rain and sunshine, night and day,
Undistinguished roll away,
Hour succeeding hour.
He heard not the music, soft yet dread,
Which the billows were making far overhead :

He saw not the fitful shadowy light
(Like the struggling moon on a cloudy night),
Which plays on many a hidden gem,
Meet for Varuna's[61] diadem.
    But on Vaikuntha's[62] lord,
    In silence best adored,
So firmly had he fixed his bosom's every chord,
  He knew no thought of weary care,
  Aye wandering through those regions fair
  Which Lakshmī's self delights to bless,—
  Lakshmī, the queen of happiness.

36.

As one who lieth bound in sleep
  In some enchanted isle,
Lulled by the sound of streams which sweep
O'er pebbly channels to the deep,—
  But he dreameth on the while:
    He rideth again
    To the battle-plain,
      As he rode in the days of old;
  He graspeth the band
  In his stalwart hand,
  And the glorious flag of his native land
      To victory doth unfold:

Or he speedeth away to a lonely tower,
And he sitteth once more in his lady's bower,
While the bright sunbeam,
Like a golden stream,
Comes floating in through the lattice high.
Where the sweet woodbine
And the jessamine
Hang in an odorous canopy.
For who wills to be free, him none shall enthrall,
Since a freedom there is which surpasseth all.
The freedom of the mind:
The tyrant's chain, and the sorcerer's charm,
May fetter the hand and unnerve the arm.
But the spirit they cannot bind.

37.

While twice twelve times the gods and manes drained
The silver bowl that radiant Soma[63] gained,
Bound in his rocky prison the prince remained.
But little the power of faith he knows
Who deems Prahlāda stilled for aye:
The rocks were rent, and the captive rose,
And breathed the air of upper day.

38.

What can heal the blindness
  Of rash and headstrong pride?
Although the king with kindness
  His son returning eyed,
Yet to the god by whom,
In his dungeon of doubt and gloom,
That son was still protected,
  His homage paid he not:
The warnings were neglected;
  The wonders all forgot.

39.

'Twas evening, and the sun was low:
  His rays of glory brightly shone
  The softly rippling waves upon,
That shorewards ceaseless flow:
  As though a stream of gold
  Its liquid treasure rolled
  To bathe the coursers seven,[64]
All weary of their race through the high vault of
    heaven.

40.

Beneath the palace gate,
With pillars wrought of antique stone,
Carved with the exploits great
Of those old kings who held the throne
Of Diti's sons,—alone
Prahlāda and the Rājā sate.
The prince perceived the sinking ray,
And rose the simple rites to pay,
Due from the pious ere the day is done.
As he went forth, his father bade him stay:
"Leave me not yet, my son,
Thy Vishnu, how can he
From far Vaikuntha see
One rite the less performed on earth?
Or is thy master so severe
That one neglect outweighs the worth
Of all good works performed through many a year?"

41.

"Who serveth Vishnu well, for love him serveth,
Not for reward," Prahlāda made reply:
"If by delusion led from right he swerveth,
To his preserver contrite let him fly.

But how can he forgiveness hope to win,
Who falls rebellious into wilful sin?
And deem not he in heaven alone abides,
Whose spirit nature's countless workings guides:
Whether in whirlwinds and in storms he rides,
Or bids the seasons roll the appointed year,—
Or whether he descends to scan
The secrets of the heart of man,
Vishnu is present here.
For know, our spirits' inmost thought
Is unto him as surely known
As act in that effulgence wrought
Which beams around his lotus throne."

42.

The king a glance of anger cast,
And on the portal's column vast
Struck down his massive mace:—
"And is he here? Then let my foe
His form disclose, that we may know
Whose might should rule the world below,
Whom serve the human race."

43.

He struck; the stone asunder flew,
And Hari's self appeared to view,
  In form of awe and dread;
No look with heavenly beauty graced,
No glance of mercy could be traced;
But, on a human body placed,
  Appeared a lion's head.
Vain was the strife, and vain escape:
Back to the chasm the fearful shape
  His struggling victim led:
  And, as the guilty spirit fled,
  On the far mountain's top the sun's last ray
    was shed.

44.

Thus the reign of evil ended:
  Thus did vengeance conquer pride:
Though he, by magic charms defended,
  Earth and heaven alike defied,
Yet was the web with craft designed
  By Vishnu's might asunder rent,
For wickedness is ever blind,
  And leaves a way for punishment.

45.

Sing we to him who shall yet return [65]
In our season of utmost need;
With a meteor flash his sword shall burn,
As he mounts on his snow-white steed.
With the hosts of the wicked he war shall wage,
A victor from shore to shore;
And the earth from the stains of the iron age
To virtue and peace restore.
For the wisdom of old in vain we seek,
Perplexed in fear and doubt,
And the hearts of men are all too weak
To work their salvation out;
And the infidel bands are increasing fast,
And the faithful oppressed and slain—
When shall the fated days be past,
And our help return again?

The Lamentation of Aja.

FROM THE RAGHUVANSHA, OR CHRONICLE OF RAGHU'S LINE.

[King Aja, son of Raghu, and grandfather of Rāma, was married to a nymph, enchanted to the form of a mortal princess. Her spell was to cease when she met the flowers of her native paradise. Accordingly, when the king and queen were walking together in the wood, Nārada[66] happened to pass, and a gust of wind carried his garland to the breast of the queen, on which she swooned and died.]

My own, my loveliest,
I clasp thee to my breast,
A lute with chords unstrung;
Hushed is thy music tone,
An evening lotus lone,
No bee to murmur deep its snowy leaves among.

Hath beauty power to slay?
Could blossoms sweet and gay
Destroy this perfect form?
Ay! softest natures oft
Death smites with weapons soft;
Snow-rills the lotus kill, which braved the pelting storm.

This wreath of vakul[67] sweet
Remaineth incomplete,
We plaited hand in hand;
Thou didst begin the rite
These graceful trees to unite,[68]
But now their yearning boughs must long unwedded stand.

The Ashoka's[69] fertile shoot,
Of thy sweet touch the fruit,
Its flowers above thee weeps;
I thought to bind thy hair
With those red blossoms fair;
How can they deck the pyre whereon my darling sleeps?

The Chakravāka[70] soon
Rejoins his mate; the moon
Brings joy once more to night:
These wait and trust, but I
Look vainly to the sky,
Which mocks my hopes with winds that wave thy ringlets light.

Thy tinkling girdle pressed
So close thy gentle breast,

It knew each secret beat;
Now on thy heart it lies,
Silent its melodies,
As though its spirit still went with its mistress sweet.

A bitter tear-mixed draught
Must by thy shade be quaffed
For wine of glad desire:
A couch of leaves new-spread
Was once too harsh a bed;
How will thy tender limbs endure the cruel pyre?

Thy voice the koïls[71] show,
Thy timid glance the doe,
To lighten my distress;
The swans thy stately pace,
The wind-waved boughs thy grace;—
But these are not my love, and I am comfortless.

My light is fled to-day;
My glory wanes away;
My state a joyless throne;
My songs henceforth have ceased:
My year is void of feast;
My brave array is lost; my couch is dark and lone.

Had I offended aught,
Thy gentle heart no thought
Of anger felt to me :
Why are my prayers unheard ?
Without one farewell word,
To leave thine only love, who never lovèd but thee !

Thy friends were true each one ;
An orbèd moon thy son ;
Thy husband, thine through life.
Oh ! what to me is left,
By death of thee bereft,
The partner of my joys, my friend, companion, wife ?

The Last Ordeal of Sītā.

[The story of Sītā, the sweetest heroine in all pagan story, should be told by a chief of poets, not a mere translator of ballads. Still, in a collection of Indian legends, it could not be altogether omitted.

Dasharatha, King of Ayodhyā (Awadh or Oudh), had, by his three wives, four sons. The eldest of these, Rāma, repaired to Mithilā (Tirhut), the court of King Janaka, who had promised the hand of Sītā—daughter of the earth, but found and adopted by him—to that competitor who should bend the bow of Shiva, which was preserved in his family. Rāma not only bent but broke it, and thereby won the princess, but also incurred the hostility of Parashu Rāma,[73] or Rāma with the axe, a warlike saint, and declared enemy of the warrior caste, of whom he saw in Rāma the champion, as well as the contemner of his patron, the god Shiva. But Rāma vanquished him, on his challenge to a trial of skill in archery, by striking a revolving mark, at which he might only aim by its reflection in a vessel of oil. On Rāma's return, he was to be inaugurated as successor to the throne; but his stepmother claimed two boons formerly promised by her husband, and selected the inauguration of her own son Bharata, and the banishment of Rāma for fourteen years. Rāma accordingly went into exile with his wife and half-brother Lakshmana, who refused to leave him. The king soon afterwards died of grief, and Bharata hastened to recall Rāma; but the latter refused to transgress the word of his dead father, so Bharata placed Rāma's shoes on the throne, governing as his vicegerent. Meanwhile, Rāma and his companions journeyed on with many adventures, and at last settled by the source of the Godāvarī, near Nāsik, the holy city of the Deccan. Here Rāvana, the ten-headed giant, who ruled Lankā, or Ceylon, and had subdued even the gods and elements to his will, beguiled both Sītā's protectors from her side by the semblance of a golden deer;

and then, presenting himself as a pilgrim perishing of thirst, persuaded her to leave the safe limits of her hut to assist him, when he carried her off to his palace. There Rāma at last discovered her, with the help of his allies, the monkeys and bears (no doubt the aboriginal tribes who inhabited the woods and hills of the south). These built Adam's Bridge, to enable him to cross the Straits; and, after several battles, Rāvana was slain, and Sitā delivered. She, however, could not be received by her husband, till she had proved her purity by the ordeal of fire, when the gods rained flowers on her, and transported the party in a heavenly car to Ayodhyā. Upon their arrival Bharata resigned the government, and they dwelt happily till Rāma, on hearing that his subjects blamed him for taking back a wife who had been so long in the power of the ravisher, determined to put her away; and when, shortly before the birth of her sons Kusha and Lava, she expressed a wish to revisit the banks of the Ganges, the scene of her first wanderings, he desired Lakshmana to leave her there. So she dwelt in the hermitage, and Rāma reigned solitary and remorseful. But, when some years after he held a great sacrifice in an assembly of all the citizens without the walls, he was attracted by the appearance of two noble youths, who sang the Rāmāyana, or history of his own exploits. On his inquiring their birth, they introduced the hermit and their mother, who proved to be his long-banished Sitā.]

Yes, Rāma, it is I; behold again
Her who was once thy wife, thy widow now,
Long years exiled from happiness and thee;
And happier those who widows are indeed,
Whom duty bids not to survive their lords,
And drag out lingering years on earth alone.
Yet am I not all cheerless in my woe:
I still may learn thy deeds, still hear thy name
A wonder and a praise on lips of men.

And I am still the mother of thy sons,
Thy sons and worthy thee,—worthy to fill
Thy throne hereafter, blessing the earth with rule.

There is no sin, no crime 'gainst God or man,
But has its penance fitted to the case,
And not to be exceeded. What for me?
Is't not enough, these weary, weary years?
Is there no memory of our early love,
And the long troubles we together bare?
Dost not remember all my joy and pride,
When sceptred kings contended for this hand,
And thou didst conquer:—and that fearful day,
When I beheld, with terror and with prayers,
How the destroyer of the warrior race
Despised thy youth and spurned thy courtesy,
But went back humbled? So, while, blest by all,
The bridal train moved home triumphantly,
There fell the cruel writ of banishment:
And thou, my noble Rāma, murmuredst not,—
Thou heldest years of poverty and toil
Less evil than to break a father's oath,
Though rashly given. Nor did I put off
The bracelets of my marriage,[73] newly bound:

I could not dwell in palaces alone,—
I, chosen by the crown of Raghu's race.[74]
By pathless ways, through woods and wilds we went;
O'er rocks and rivers, and the haunts of beasts,
Supported by thy love, I journeyed on.
And oh! how happy was our woodland life,—
To weave thy forest garb, to dress thy meal,
To rest in peace while sweet Godāvarī
Lulled us with murmurs down her rocky bed!
Oh, that thou wert a simple forester,
And I thy love! Thy love? I am thy love,
And thou the noblest king that ruleth right,
And meteth justice to a hundred tribes.
Then would I rob thee of thy high estate,
And leave the nations to a meaner lord?
So were their slanders true, mine exile just;
For no true wife is she, though chaste and pure.
Who loves herself before her husband's fame.

Yes, I transgressed; was it so grave a crime?
I could not see him perishing for thirst,
An old, frail man, and clad in holy weeds.
I thought not of thy warning, and the wiles
Of that deceiver, source of all our woe.

I crossed the safe enclosure of our hut.
Then straight the giant showed his monstrous form :
He seized me, calling vainly on thy name,
And bore me trembling o'er the hills away.
The savage dwellers in the woods and caves
Took pity on my grief ; they marked my path ;
They crossed the mountains and the southern sea ;
They found me prisoned in the Ashoka [75] grove,
And ranged their hosts 'neath thine avenging arm.

Then came the moment of thy victory,
When I was clasped to thy triumphant breast :
Thou dost remember that ! But yet thou saidst,
"I know thy heart mine own ; I know thine eyes,
That could not look thus bravely into mine,
Had aught of ill befallen ; yet, sweet heart,
The wife of Rāma must be stainless proved
In sight of gods and men." Then I replied,
"Rāma, thou speakest well ; dear to a wife
Should be her husband's honour as her own ;
Wherefore prepare the fiery ordeal,—
My love and truth shall bear me fearless through."
I went ; I thought but of thy love and thee :
The gods took pity on mine innocence,

And rained down blossoms from no earthly trees.
So passed I pure in sight of gods and men.

How sweet, my love, was then our homeward way!
A double brightness glittered on the waves;
A double beauty blossomed in the woods;
The spring leaped up at once to sudden life;
The sun shone fearless, and the wind blew free,
Since thou hadst overthrown the evil one.
The grateful breezes wafted home our car;
O'er sunlit seas we crossed, o'er coral caves,
O'er wave-kissed rocks, and bays with fringe of palm.
We passed wild hills, the haunt of savage tribes;
Bright rivers flashing through embowering woods;
And lakes, the home of reed-frequenting cranes.
We watched the altars smoke from forest glades,
Where holy hermits watered tender shrubs,
And strewed wild rice before their fostered fanes.
We marked our silent hut, and that tall tree
Which spreads its branches set with ruby fruit,[76]
Where Yamunā leaps blue to Gangā's arms.
And last we crossed rich plains and fertile fields:
Far off we marked Ayodhyā's gleaming walls,
And, by the dust which rose between, we knew

Thy brother led his host to welcome us,
And render up the throne he kept so well.

Did I unmeekly bear our royal state?
The citizens stand round:—I call on each,
Yea, on my slanderers, to answer me.
Was I not gracious to the lowliest?
Did I not ever seek affliction out,
To comfort where I might? I grudged thee not
To cares of governance and days of toil;
I strove to cheer thee in thine hours of ease,
Sending thee back from leisure well refreshed
To drag once more the heavy yoke of rule.
But thou,—when under show of humouring
My lightest wish, thou sentest me abroad,
Fell on my ears that knell, "Return no more!"
Had I then disobeyed thy will, or heard
With murmuring? Not one word to speak farewell!
Never to look upon thy children's face!
Oh! it was cruel, bearing this from thee.
Yet thou didst love me once. Why dost thou turn
Thy face away, and answer not a word?
Is there no hope that time may change my doom?
Ṛāma, thou dost not doubt me in thy heart,

But thou dost fear the people; 'tis for kings
To lead the people, not be led by them:
For kings are set by God before the world,
His chiefest servants of created men,
To govern right by conscience and by laws,
Holding a perfect mirror to the tribes.
Thou wouldst not stoop to sin through fear of death;
Why persecute the guiltless, break thy vows,
Through fear of tarnishing thy mortal fame?
'Twere worthier of a hero and a king
To do the right through shame and through disgrace.
  Thou sayest, "Clear thyself before the eyes
Of this assembly; then thrice welcome home."
Yet what so clear but time may veil with doubt?
And what so pure but slander may assail?
  Well, if thou wilt, there is no other way;—
O Earth, my mother, on whose silent breast
I lay a helpless child, when the good king
Found me and fostered me,—hear thou my prayer!
If never I—in thought, or word, or act—
Transgressed my marriage duty and my vows
To my loved husband, take me once again
To thy kind bosom, hushing me to rest
From all the troubles of this weary world.

Then o'er the people passed a murmuring wave,
As when a sudden gust shakes the dry trees
Which pant for rain after a sultry day;
And Rāma cried a loud and bitter cry,
And started from his seat; but, as he came,
She, with her eyes still fixed upon his face,—
As a tired lily sinks beneath the wave,
Its day's work done,—sank, and was seen no more.

Sharmishthā.

Fair is the city of gold that floats in the fields of heaven,
Ruled by the Dānava chiefs, the kings of the Titans of old:
After the shower of summer is brushed from a smiling even,
Far through the clearness of air is it given those walls to behold.

City of golden ramparts that blaze in the sun at his setting,
Flashing with banners of crimson and amber changing to green;
Silver and diamond turrets of marvellous mystical fretting,
Deep in the lap of the cloud by the lightning momently seen.

Fair are the fields of the city, with pleasant murmur of waters,
Bright with lovelier blossoms than gardens of earth can bear;
Fairer the stately forms of the mighty Dānava's daughters:
Fairest Sharmishthā, the princess who leads that company fair.

Was it a childish quarrel, a thrust, a tumult of falling?
  Close in the weeds at their side lay hidden the ruinous well:
Devayānī's name in sudden alarm they are calling—
  Hush! but no reply is heard from the pit where she fell.

Scattered for help they fly toward the distant walls of the city:
  What shall the maiden do, returned again from her swoon?
Faint with terror and pain she cries for assistance and pity,
  Left in her wild despair to die in misery soon.

Who comes riding here, a king in the port of his glory?
  Rājā of rājās he, Yayāti of matchless might:
Bright doth his name shine forth in the annals of India's story,
  Bright as the flag of his car in the stormiest billows of fight.

King Yayāti hears the cry of the frantic maiden;
  Strong is his bow-worn arm to help with tenderest skill:
Swift to the city he guides the car with its sweet freight laden;
  Safe in her father's arms he leaves her trembling still.

Wroth was Shukra[77] the sage: he stood in the palace of meeting:
  Famous in council or war, the chiefs sat each in his place:
"Art thou distraught, O king,[78] that thou choosest a fortune so fleeting,
  Mocking thy teacher thus with an outrage wrought to his race?

"I, whose will controls the loveliest planet of morning—
  I, who in direst straits have proved to safety your guide—
How were your homes a prey and your walls to the Suras a scorning,[79]
  Should I in anger depart and leave you alone in your pride!"

Sore dismay in the breasts of the chiefs his threatening engendered:
  Long with entreaties they strove to abate the force of his ire:
"Let the source of the wrong as a slave to my daughter be rendered;
  Only thus may ye hope to avert the curse of her sire."

Who comes riding back, a king in the pomp of his splendour?
King Yayāti comes, a prosperous wooing to speed.
Devayānī, his bride, is fair and loving and tender,
Trusting the strong right arm that helped her so well in her need.

Answered Shukra the sage, as the homeward march was beginning—
Elephants, chariots, steeds with royal and bridal state—
"Blest in thy prowess, O son, be thou blest in the wife thou art winning,
Worthy in soul as in form, with a lord of the earth to mate.

"If she suffice thee not, there are royal maids for thy wooing;
Noblest and fairest, each would joy to stand at thy side:
But, unless blinded by passion thou rush to thine own undoing,
Choose not amongst her slaves to vex the soul of thy bride."

Swiftly the seasons go by in valour and kingly duty,
  Measuring justice to each, and leading to conquest the brave;
Swiftly the years glide away, to love, and splendour and beauty;
  Slowly the months drag on which link the chains of the slave.

Patient and humble, Sharmishthā, her fault with meekness redeeming,
  Daily with duteous hand fulfils the hests of the queen:
Only, when evening reveals her home in its golden seeming,
  Silent her tears flow down in the thought of the days that have been.

Sweet is the season of spring and the smile of the jasmine bower;
  Pleasant the plash of the fountain that drops so cool from above;
Soothing the songs of the birds, that welcome the mango flower
  Blossoming newly to point the sharpest arrow of love.[80]

Noon[81] from the palace gate by the warder is duly
chanted;
Wearied from judgment the king is gone to the alleys
green :
Who is the maid more fair than the loveliest flower there
planted,
Tending through sultry heat the trees that are dear to
the queen?

Was it strange that the damsel ere long had a royal
lover?[82]
Was it strange that her heart by so gallant a wooer
was won?
Well was their secret kept, nor did Shukra the marriage
discover
Till to a princely youth was grown Sharmishthā's son.

Out spake Shukra the sage who rules the planet of
morning,—
Still in his bosom rankled the insult done to his child—
"Hast thou dared my curse, nor heeded my words of
warning,
Reckless in thirst of pleasure, and through thy passion
beguiled?

"Suddenly then thine age shall arrive ere thy prime is completed,
Manhood turn to decay, and strength be wasted and dead."
Devayānī the queen in vain her father entreated:
"Yes! if the weight of my curse his son will bear in his stead."

"Hearken, Yadu[83] my first-born, my pride, and the heir of my power,
Art thou willing to bow thy neck to the load of thy sire?"
"Father, the bud of my youth but now is opening to flower;
How can I thus resign each hope of my life's desire?"

Then the rest of the princes their father's summons collected;
Hoping relief from the curse, he prayed them one by one;
Loving the pleasures of youth they all his entreaty rejected,—
All but the youngest, Puru,[84] the gentle Sharmishthā's son.

"Father, thy will is my law," so answered he cheerful-
hearted,
"Father, my life is thy gift, and I render thee back
thine own."
Bowed with decay in his youth, he forth from the presence
departed;
Royal in manhood's pride Yayātī sat on his throne.

Long he reigned in glory, enjoying each lawful pleasure,
Till he had learnt how the gladness of earth is with
bitterness blent:
Then having vowed with his queens to seek for heavenly
treasure,
Back to his son he rendered the youth so willingly lent.

"Meed of thy patience and love, in my seat, O Puru, I
crown thee;
Thee shall thy brethren serve, and rule their realms in
thy name;
High in the roll of the mighty shall prowess and justice
renown thee,
Higher the weakness thou barest ennoble thy household
fame."

Ambā.

["I will not do as Ambā, the daughter of Indradawan, king of the city of Kāshī,[85] did, who left her husband and went to King Bhīsham; and, when he would not retain her, returned to her husband; and again, when her husband expelled her, sate down on the bank of the Gangā, and performed a great penance to Mahādev; and, when Bholānāth[86] came and gave her whatever boon she asked, went, in the strength of that boon, and revenged herself on King Bhīsham; this I cannot do."—Eastwick's Translation of the *Prem Sāgar*.[87]]

1.

Ah me! it is a weary thing
  To love, and love the lost;
To see the fairest bud of spring
  Nipped by a chilling frost;
And all that once would pleasure bring,
Jar on the soul, like Vīnā's[88] string
  By sudden discord crossed:
To feel the soul of gladness die away;
Sad when among the sad,—more sad among the gay.
  Yet time the deepest wounds can heal,
  And bosoms seared may cease to feel;

And Hope her wildest raptures sings
Amongst the world of shadowy things.
Then may the heart elastic rise
  Beneath a load of care,
And dream of one amid the skies,
  Who waits our coming there;
  Of one who doth a pleasant bower prepare
Nigh where his own blest spirit lies,
And to the god of many eyes,[89]
  Who rules those gardens fair,
Borne on the fragrant breeze above,
  Breathes forth one earnest prayer:
  One drop to fill the cup of bliss,
  One joy there lacketh yet,—and this
Is union with the soul we love.

2.

A weary thing it is to love,—
  To love, and not be loved again;
To feel the heart that fain would rove,
  Enthralled by Passion's iron chain.
When Hope, that soars on pinion bold,
  Falls from her dizzy venture soon,
Rewarded with a glance as cold
  As that poor bird which woos the moon.[90]

But I, in childhood's golden morn
 With regal splendour nursed,
Must dwell an outcast and forlorn,
 In deepest woe immersed;
And in the mouths of men unborn
Be held a byword and a scorn,
 Of all my race accursed.
My wealth, my grandeur, and my name,
My crown, my bridegroom, and my fame,
My earthly happiness, my hopes of heaven,
All, all my treasures I for this return have given.

3.

I sat me down on Gangā's brink,
 Beside the sacred stream;
I sat me down, and strove to think,
 For all was as a dream;
And that which I had said and done did seem
 The fragments of a half-forgotten lay,
 Sung by the bards of old on some high festal day.
I looked within, and all my brain did burn;
I looked toward home, and how could I return?
I looked to him, and found no pity there;
A loathing for my love, a scorn for my despair.

Beware, and rue thee of thy bearing high;
Love, watered with a smile, can never die;
But springs there from its scathed and blasted root
A plant of swiftest growth, and Vengeance is its
fruit.

4.

Day and night, through many a year,
There I kept my penance drear;
Cold and heat,
And storm and sleet,
Steadfast still I held my seat,
Bark my robe, and herbs my meat;—
Such the vow to Shiva dear.

5.

It was a night
As soft and bright
As the times when I was young;
When, beneath the shade
Which the banian made,
To the Vīnā's chords I sung;
The sun's last rays
With a crimson blaze

Lit up the skiff's white sail;
And a thousand flowers
From the jasmine bowers
Breathed on the evening gale.
All was moveless and still and calm,
Save the wind as it sighed through the groves of palm,
And the fireflies flickering 'midst the trees,—
One scarce might know them from stars, I ween,
Dancing the blackening waves between,
When the ripples are rising before the breeze.
All was hushed, save the insect's hum,
And the plash of the measured oar,
And the boatman's song, and the distant drum
From the feast on the farther shore.
Then a burning thought
Of the sorrow I wrought
Like lightning crossed my brain;
And my vengeance slept;
And my soul had wept,
And my curse been recalled again;
But I remembered my hate and my vow,
I remembered my scorn and my pain;
My heart, though it break, to my will shall bow;—
So I turned to my penance again.

6.

Soon as the whirlwind of passion passed,
The heaven with clouds was overcast;
Huge and black from the south they came,
And the lightning wrote on them its lines of flame.
With the dim-seen shapes of a spirit band,
And fiendish laughter on either hand,
  That drowned the rising storm,
Borne on a bull as the snow-wreath white,[91]
Revealed by the flashes of sudden light,
  I marked a godlike form:
By the living serpent his waist around,
By the collar of skulls his neck that bound,
  By his throat with its deep-blue ring,[92]
By his glance of terror and majesty,
By his moonèd brow and his triple eye,
  I knew the mountain-king.
Came there a voice; it seemed not loud,
Yet deep as the distant thunder-cloud;
Still was all else, and hushed the storm,
But I could not gaze on that fearful form,
  So before his feet I bowed.

7.

"Well hast thou striven, worshipper mine,
Striven 'gainst feelings of mortal birth;
They who would rise to power divine
Must crush the weakness that springs from earth.
Well hast thou served me, worshipper mine;
Take thou the boon that thy heart desires;
The Swarga[93] king shall his throne resign,
If to dominion thy soul aspires.
Seekest thou riches, worshipper mine?
Seekest thou fortune unharmed by fate?
Kuvera[94] shall yield thee his treasures nine,
And Lakshmī's[95] self as thy handmaid wait.
Seekest thou vengeance, worshipper mine?
Such is the joy that thy soul would know?
Have then thy will; he is thine, he is thine,
And thy curses shall drag him to ruin and woe!"

8.

He ceased; and, with a crash the sky that rent,
And through the echoing clouds rolled far away,
As chafing that their wrath so long was pent,
What time a mightier power bade it stay,

Rejoicing now to give their anger vent,
  The thunder-spirits joined in fierce affray;
And to and fro the fitful lightning went,
  And the rain poured in torrents where I lay:
    Yet I lay still.
"And mine," I cried, "is now the power,
  And he must bend him to my will:
Say, will he scorn me now, in my triumphal hour?"
And still I lay, until the tempest rude,
  Borne on the wings of night, passed slow away;
And the new sun with gold the waters strewed,
  And birds came forth to greet the early day:
And still my thoughts on those same themes would
    brood,
  Nor once did towards the path of mercy stray.—
Then up I rose, ere yet the sun was high,
  And to the town I took my weary way:
Few knew me there, I ween, so wan and changed was I.

The Story of the Syamantak Jewel.

[The story of the Syamantak jewel is found in all the histories of Krishna, but not placed in its proper order among the incidents of his life. It appears to be a legend much older than the rest, coming down from the time when Krishna was no demi-god, but merely a hero, of marvellous prowess indeed, but one who fell into disgrace and formed erroneous opinions, like ordinary mortals. There are many arguments in favour of the opinion that his divine character is partly founded on some spurious gospel. His name is pronounced Krishta, or Krista; and in many of the events of his life there are resemblances to the sacred narrative, too remarkable for accidental coincidence.

A simple ballad style seems most suitable to this curious legend of ancient manners. The independence and importance of the ladies introduced is one proof of its antiquity.]

Part I.

Long did Satrājit serve the Sun;
A boon of price from the god he won:—

"Grant the Syamantak gem, O King;
Honour and wealth will its presence bring."

"Honour and wealth to the pure 'twill give,
But none save the chaste can hold and live."

He came with the gem to the Yādavas' hall;
Up rose the princes and warriors all.

"Hearken, O Krishna, thy fame has spread;
The sun-god visits thy roof," they said.

Forth looked Krishna; laughing he spake,
"Syamantak's lustre ye here mistake."

Answered the Yādavas, mickle of might,
"Such prize for Satrājit is all unright.

"The jewel is meet for a king to gain;
Take it, O Krishna, for Ugrasen." [96]

Out laughed Krishna, playing of dice;—
"Hearest, Satrājit, the chiefs' advice?"

Up rose Satrājit, silent and vexed;
He went to his home with his heart perplexed.

Answered Prasena, the hunter rude,—
"Brother, why sittest so gloomy of mood?"

"Krishna is wroth with our house, I wot;
He asked me a gift, and I gave it not."

Prasena rose, and the gem he took;
He went to the wood with an angry look.

Ranging the wood on his snorting steed,
A lion slew them, as fate decreed.

Syamantak he bare to his darksome den;
It seemed as the sun had entered then;

The innermost depths were all ablaze;
The vaults reflected on the rays;

To the realms below their way they made,
Where Jāmbavat, king of the bears, was laid.

He rose in wrath from his gloomy lair;
"Who troubles my rest with this wondrous glare?"

He searched till he came to the upper ground;
The lion he smote, whom first he found;

The gem as a trophy he carried away,
And hung it on high for his child to play.

Long did his comrades seek Prasen;
They searched for him thrice, but they searched in vain.

Satrājit tossed on his sleepless bed;
"What troubles thy rest?" his lady said.

"Peace, good wife, let thy tongue be still;
Who trusteth a woman, he fareth ill;

"No secret stays in a woman's skin;
She tells abroad what she hears within."

Many and ready the tears she shed;
"As thou lovest me not, thou shalt see me dead.

"Am I like others, my word to break?"
She wearied her lord, till thus he spake:—

"Krishna is wroth with our house, I wot;
He asked me a gift, and I gave it not.

"It fears me now he has met Prasen,
Has taken the jewel, and him has slain.

"But see that my thought to none thou tell;
God knoweth whether it so befell."

Little the lady slept that night;
She sprang from her couch at dawn of light.

"Hasten, my slaves, our neighbours call;
Send for my friends and companions all.—

"Krishna is wroth with our house, I wot;
He asked us a gift, and we gave it not.

"Now in the wood he has met Prasen,
Has taken the jewel, and him has slain.

"My lord has told me; be sure 'tis true;
But tell not the secret I trust to you."

In silence her friends amazed withdrew;
They talked of the matter by three and by two.

On Krishna's head they cast the blame:
Astonished was he when he heard the same.

"Hearken, O chiefs, and Ugrasen;
I needs must clear me of this foul stain."

With a chosen band he searched around;
At length the horse's track he found;

First the horse and stout Prasen;
Last they came on the lion slain.

Sore afraid were the Yādavs brave;
None but Krishna would enter the cave.

"Some mighty monster must here abide;
Rush not on certain death," they cried.

"Witness how died Prasen, we bear:
Clear is thy fame; why further dare?"

Answered them Krishna:—"I rest not yet;
On the missing jewel my heart is set.

"Await my return for days but ten;
I come as a victor, or come not again."

Into the terrible cave he pressed;
He groped his path with dauntless breast.

Far off he saw Syamantak's ray;
Down to the depths he made his way.

The gem above the cradle hung;
Forward, with eager face, he sprung.

Jāmbavat roused at the infant's cries;
They rushed together with kindling eyes.

They grappled as heroes grappled of yore;
They wrestled for fourteen days and more.—

But, when ten days were gone and past,
Home went the Yādavas overcast.

"What fight could there be, so long unwon?
The days of Krishna are told and done."

The rites of the Shrāddha[97] they duly paid,
Albeit no corpse on the pile was laid.

The food, for his spirit's refreshing meant,
New life to the fainting Krishna lent.

Both had been weary and weak with fight;
Krishna sprang up with redoubled might.

Jāmbavat craves for quarter now;—
"Surely of Rāma's race art thou:

"I warred in Lankā,[98] with Rāma's men,
'Gainst Rāvan the curst, with his faces ten.

"None since that day has equalled my strength;
A second Rāma I view at length."

He feasted Krishna with royal cheer;
He plighted the hand of his daughter dear.

Syamantak in dower he likewise gave;
He sent them safe from the mountain cave.

Glad of heart came Krishna down;
With Jāmbavatī he reached the town.

He gave Satrājit the jewel free:—
"Take thou thine own, and blame not me."

Home went Satrājit, bowed with shame;
With anxious mind to his wife he came:—

"Wherewith can we this wrong repair?"
"Give Satyabhāmā, our daughter fair."

A lucky time did the Brāhman name;
The family priest to Krishna came.

With rice unground on a dish were put
Forehead-paint, a rupee, and a cocoa-nut.

Where all the guests and Brāhmans sat,
Came Krishna, in bridegroom's high-peaked hat.

He circled round with his bride in hand;
From her slender wrist he loosed the band.

She sat on his left, in her place beside;
They returned the board, and the knot untied.

In robes of honour the bards they arrayed;
To the family goddess their vows they paid.

Rice-milk and sugar in sport they ate;
All things were done as the Veds dictate.

A dowry rich did Satrājit tell;
They left him with music and mirth as well.

Syamantak among his gifts he sent:
With that was Krishna not content:—

"The jewel thou givest was gained from the Sun,
But we receive *gifts* from no gods but One."

Part II.

Kritavarman and Akrūr took this ill;
They sought Shatadhanwan, the feeble of will.

"We courted Satrājit's daughter both,
And her father to thee did the maid betroth.

"Are we so base, to be held for nought?
Or has Krishna, the cowherd, the kingdom bought?

"Now, in his absence, Satrājit kill;
Under wrongs like thine can a man be still?

"Nor Krishna nor Rāma[99] will soon be near;
And, should they be wroth, thy friends are here."

Shatadhanwan the witless at night took sword;
The jewel he seized, and smote its lord.

Satyabhāmā heard, and arose in haste;
Her father's corpse in oil she placed.

Filled with fury she mounted her car;
Day and night she travelled afar.

In Hastināpur[100] her lord she found;
The Kaurava[101] princes were seated around.

The eyes of Krishna flashed with flame:
"Cease from thy bitter weeping, dame.

"My wrath is kindled without thy wail;
Who spoils the nests must the tree assail.

"Hear, Balarāma! dead is Prasen;
Now is Satrājit foully slain.

"So is Syamantak our common right;
With me then against Shatadhanwan fight."

Shatadhanwan heard, and was sore afraid;
He sought Kritavarman, imploring aid.

Laughed Kritavarman, the crafty and cool:
"The wise man *counsels; acts* the fool.

"Can I with Krishna and Rām contend?
They who are strongest find *me* their friend."

Shatadhanwan heard, and was sore dismayed;
He went to Akrūra, imploring aid.

His hands he bound with his turban-cloth,—
"Hide me, O sage, from Krishna's wrath."

Answered Akrūra, the placid of mind,—
"Why didst thou listen, and look not behind?

"Life is dear to the wise man's heart:
Why should *I* die, by taking thy part?"

Shatadhanwan heard, and sadly sighed,—
"This fatal gem thou at least wilt hide?"

"So far will I help thee, if sworn thou art
Not even in death to betray my part."

On his swiftest mare Shatadhanwan fled;
A hundred leagues in a day she sped.

Krishna harnessed his coursers four;
He followed with Rāma, still gaining more.

When they were come by Mithilā [102] town,
Faint and dying the mare dropped down.

"The ground is bad; with the car stay thou:
On foot," quoth Krishna, "I follow him now."

Two kos[103] in vain Shatadhanwan fled:
The disc[104] of Krishna smote his head.

The body and dress he searched around;
He returned ashamed; no jewel he found.

"Brother, our quest is all in vain;
No jewel I find on the caitiff slain."

Wroth was Rāma,—"Shame on thy brow;
I wot no brother of mine art thou.

"False of tongue, and greedy of gain,
Go where thou wilt, our paths are twain."

Home went Krishna, sad and distraught;
Satrājit forth from the oil he brought.

Duly he paid the rites of fire;
With his own right hand he lighted the pyre.—

Long years in health and plenty passed ;
Balarāma returned, appeased at last.

Doubtful in heart was Akrūr the sage ;
He went from the city on pilgrimage.

Soon as the jewel was carried out,
Came on the city disease and drought.

Answered the Yādavas, mickle of might,—
" Whence is this sickness, famine, and blight ?

" Akrūra is born of a holy race ;
His presence it was that preserved the place.

" We will bring him back by an embassage,
And to hold him scathless our faith will gage."

Soon as Akrūr returned from the east,
Plagues and portents and famine ceased.

Krishna mused at the altered state,—
" Akrūra's virtue was ne'er so great ! "

He feasted the chiefs in his palace hall;
He spake to Akrūra before them all,—

"As do thy virtues, thy riches abound;
We know that Syamantak *thou* hast found.

"Keep it, and guard the city from ill;
But show it, for Rāma mistrusts me still."

Akrūra wist not what to reply;—
"They will search me and find it, if now I deny.—

"Yes, I have kept it with trouble and care;
Till the owner shall claim it, safely I bear.

"Little the holder tastes of ease;
Take it, and give it to whom thou please."

From a box of gold the gem he drew;
The sun himself they seemed to view.

Eagerly Rāma rose, and cried,—
"Remember thy word, and the gem divide."

Out and spake Satyabhāma fair,—
" The gem was my father's, and *I* am heir."

Beset was Krishna on either part,
As an ox between the wheels of the cart.

One mode he saw to end the strife,—
" We have no will for a hermit's life.

" Why should we risk the evil fate?
Wear it, Akrūra, and save the state."

He took the gem at the chief's command,
And honour and wealth it brought the land.

Rukminī.

[Rukminī was betrothed by her brother to Shishupāla, though her father wished to give her to Krishna. Rukminī sent tidings of these events to Krishna, who came and carried her off on the marriage-day.

1.

And will he come? far, far away
  Stand Vasudeva's[105] princely halls,
And distant far the white waves play
  Around the Ocean-city's[106] walls;
And many a wild and trackless wood,
  Where nought but monstrous shapes is seen,
And rock and desert many a rood,
  And hostile cities, lie between.

2.

The sceptred kings of Bharat's[107] land
  Pay homage to the lord of earth:
Why should he deign to seek the hand
  Of one whose kinsmen mock his birth?

The proudest chiefs of Manu [108] born
  Invite the lord of Yadu's [109] name;
But he must meet with hate and scorn,
  If here his promised bride he claim.

3.

Of all the royal maids of earth,
  Whose fathers rule from sea to sea,—
My peers in beauty and in birth,—
  Why should he fix his thoughts on me?
But he the sons of men excels;
  My heart he made his captive soon;
The moon sees many Bartavelles,
  The Bartavelle [110] no second moon.

4.

I waited at the lattice high;
  I listened for his courser's feet;
And joyful faces passed me by,—
  Glad voices echoed through the street.
The sound of mirth and revelry
  Came forth into the moonlit night,
And lordly strains of minstrelsy
  That tell of some old famous fight.

5.

With voice of music and of song,
O'er silken carpets, down the street,
The gay procession moved along,
The bridegroom's haughty train to meet.
The banners floated from the towers,
The city shone in all her pride;
The stately gates were wreathed with flowers,
And all were glad—except the bride.

6.

But see! the morn, the marriage morn,
Is lightening in the eastern sky;
Oh, that I were the meanest born
In the gay throng that hurry by!
If Krishna come, for him I fear,
Unaided in the unequal strife;
Yet, if no help from him be near,
A dreary lot is mine through life.

The Destruction of the Yādavas.

Part I.

The Glory of Dwārakā.

1.

Sadly sigh thy waves, O Sea,
  Along the barren sand,
Telling a mournful history
  To the lone and wasted land;
A history that endeth not
  Of sin, and shame, and woe;
Such is man's never-failing lot
  In this blind world below.
Absence and sorrow, pain and death,
  Are fated from our birth;
Such portion each inheriteth
  Who breathes the air of earth.

2.

Yet it seems me now they sing
  Than their wont a sadder song;
Sadder embassage they bring,
  In a music deep and strong,—
  Each pursuing wave along
Chanted from the coralled ring
Of the city of their king,—
  Each one, as it hurries by,
To the rock-clefts whispering.
  Then, o'er all the pools that lie
  Mirroring the clouds and sky,
Sheltered in their rocky bed
By the towering cliffs o'erhead,
Slow and solemn murmurs spread,
  As amid the grass that waves
  Over long-neglected graves,
In some city of the dead
  (Where they slumber, kings and slaves,
Side by side, unreckonèd,)
  Or the mounds that crest the plain,
  Piled above the foully slain.

3.

Even thus, in days of yore,
Sighed they to the foamy shore,
All the billows, trouble tost,
  With a sobbing motion,
Mourning o'er the treasures lost [111]
  Of the rifled ocean.
Now no mountain's circling sweep
  Gods and demons league to ply;
Now the secrets of the deep,
  As of old, untroubled lie;
  Now on pearl-adornèd beds
Ocean's powers may careless sleep;
  From the toiling serpent's heads
  Now no flaming poison spreads:
Wherefore then so mournfully
Roll thy long blue waves, O Sea?

4.

'Tis a heavier loss they weep,
All the spirits of the deep;

Weep the City of the West,[112]
Land of love, and land of rest,
'Mid the holy holiest :
  Her glory for one brief hour to see,
  One moment within her walls to be,
Was to dwell for ever blest.
More precious far such boon would be
Than all the gifts bestowed by thee,
    O Kalpa [113] tree,
Granter of every wish,—or thine,
O Surabhi,[114] of race divine,
    Mother of kine.

5.

At Krishna's word, she was reared in a night
  By the builder of Swarga's towers,[115]
The sons of Yadu [116] to shield in flight
  From the threats of the demon powers.
    They laid them down
    In the leaguered town,
  In fear of the barbarous host;
    But they roused them from sleep
    'Mid the murmurs deep
  Of the waves on their refuge-coast.

She sat as a queen
On the waters green,
Where the ocean humbly bore her;
And day and night
Sudarshan's [117] might
Kept watch and ward before her.
Well watered lay her fertile land,
Stretched far around;
Beyond, her guardian hills did stand
With forests crowned.
Yet the town wore
A glory more
A thousand-fold,—
Her jewelled halls,
Whose lofty walls
Were wrought with gold:
Where the sun shone
Her towers upon,
What eye might gaze?
In joy and mirth
Too bright for earth
Passed all her days.
Her royal state
May none relate;

So fair a spot
The eye of heaven
Through the regions seven [118]
Beholdeth not.

6.

The aged monarch still
A righteous sceptre swayed; [119]
The tribes his every will
Right cheerfully obeyed.
The chief in rank and age
Spoke words of counsel sage;
Ready with shield and brand
Did countless warriors stand.
All her priests were pure of life;
All her people void of strife;
Day by day their joy increased;
House to house was nightly feast;
Rich the wares in mart and road;
Fair the gifts on bards bestowed;
Still did vessels chased in gold
Five mysterious branches hold; [120]
Fresher garlands still were hung;
Newer praises still were sung;

Seer and sage salvation's road
From the mystic precepts showed;
Daily were the Vedas read;
For the poor the board was spread;
Never was a rite neglected;
Never was a face dejected;
Where the feet of Krishna rest,
Who could dwell, and be unblest?

Part II.

The Songs of the Bards.

7.

Evermore the tales were told,
Wonders of the times of old,—
Vishnu's gracious works of yore,
When he sought the earth before;
Yet Krishna's praises from their tongue
  Still flowed the readiest,—
And, when of Krishna's deeds they sung,
  The crowd more eager prest.

They sang the song of his wondrous birth; [121]
How the rod of the tyrant crushed the earth;
How her cry went up to the lotus-throne, [122]
And the ears of the merciful heard her groan;
How he left the dwelling of life and light
  No sage may reach in thought;
How an infant bore the preserver's might,
And mortal became the Infinite;
  So love and mercy wrought.

8.

They sang the song [123] of his childhood bright;
How he was born in the silent night;
How a mighty sleep on the warders fell,
And burst were the bars of the dungeon cell;
Rolled the thunder, and swelled the gale,
Lest the foemen should hear his first feeble wail:
  Yamunā [124] curbed her foaming tide,
    And gently kissed the shore,
  That the father might pass from side to side,
    With the precious freight he bore.
  For, though he was born in princely state,
  He left the abodes of the earthly great;

Through the forest-wilds he loved to roam,
And with simple herdsmen he made his home,
  Pursued by the demons' hate.
And, when the appointed days were past,
  And mercy ceased to plead,—
When the stroke of justice fell at last,
  And the suffering poor were freed,—
He took not the crown which his arm had won,
  But honoured his father's will,
That never of Yadu's[125] seed a son
  Should spring the throne to fill.

9.

They sang how to sea-borne Dwārakā he bore his brides away,
From the ranks of the rival suitors, and the kings in their fierce array;
They sang of the love of Rukminī,[126] and the deeds of her marriage-day,
And of the wild and wondrous cave where Jāmbavatī lay;
  How in her virgin grace he won
  Her, the daughter of the sun,

Dwelling in her magic home
Beneath the silver wave,
Till, a weary world to save,
The promised bridegroom come.

10.

Where the deep blue waters glide[127]
By the lonely river-side,
With a stately step she trod,
Like the daughter of a god :
Bright her brow as the autumn moon,[128]—
Black her locks as the clouds of June,—
Round her neck as the ring-dove's throat,—
Sweet her voice as the koïl's[129] note,—
Slender her waist as the lion's mate,—
Stately her pace as the elephant's gait,—
Dark her hair as the long black snake,—
Lovely her hands as the pride of the lake,—
Graceful her arm as the creeper's shoot,—
Ruddy her lips as the vimba's[130] fruit,—
Golden her face as the champaka's[131] hue,—
Blushing her cheeks as the rosebud new,—[132]
Smooth her limbs as the plantain's stem,—
Piercing her eyes as the polished gem,—

White her teeth as the jasmine's smile,—[133]
Strong in her beauty a saint to beguile.

11.

For her sweeter breath the bees
Left the blossoms of the trees,
Fairer though they bloomed awhile
In the sunshine of her smile.
Every rival shrub a wreath
  Flung upon her lovely head;
At her touch, its leaves beneath
  Flashed the Ashoka's[134] glowing red.
Often with her lute she wandered,
  Striking in so wild a key,
As with spirit rapt she pondered
  On her wondrous destiny,
That the timid forest-deer,[135]
  All with eyes undaunted
(Eyes so large, yet not a peer
Unto hers they stayed to hear),
  Stood with limbs implanted,
Panting, panting, ever near,
Gazing, gazing, without fear,
  By that strain enchanted.

Then the trees, whose waving tresses
Wantoned to the wind's caresses,
Cast the promise of their fruit
As a tribute to her lute,
While the koïl's chorus rang,
Answering music as she sang.

12.

The Song of Kālindī.

"How long, O father mine,[136]
Must I all lonely pine,
And waste my brightest years in solitude,
And watch the seasons range
In slow unvarying change,
Traced by their silent steps along the leafy wood?
I weary of the language of the birds:
They, mate with mate, and kind with kind. rejoice;
I weary of my own unanswered voice;
I weary of the echo whence my words
In mocking sympathy repeated came;
I weary most to see thee ever shine,
Day after day, unchangeably the same:
How long dwell I alone, how long, O father mine?

13.

"Oh, but for one brief hour, that I might hear
The speech of man, though strange the words and cold,—
And, oh, that that bright morn were dawning near,
When I shall smiles of love again behold,
And listen to that voice to fancy dear,—
Dear to my fancy, though as yet unknown
To this dull earthly sense, whose gentlest tone
Strikes chords within my breast which it can wake alone!

14.

"O Krishna, my belovèd, would that I
Were worthier of thee! I, from eldest time,
By fate predestined to such rank sublime!
And do I murmur at the months' delay,
And that my lot in nerveless rest should fall?
Though years in penance dread went lingering by,
And nights of watching closed the fasting day,
One hour of happiness were worth it all,—
One smile of thine would lives of pain repay.

15.

"Each hath his work to do, whate'er our lot,
Whate'er our calling here; and thou, my sire,
Thou readest me a lesson unforgot;
Thou castest not a glance of fond desire
Where towering Meru[137] rises, streaked with gold,
And all the gods their courts of pleasaunce hold,—
Nor toward the luscious gardens of the south,
Where all day long the softest breezes stray,—
Nor speedest, ere the destined close of day,
To quench in ocean's streams thy coursers' drouth;
But steadfast in thy march thou hold'st thine ordered way.

16.

"Each hath his work to do, the small, the great;
Not for themselves do monarchs wear the crown,
Yoked to the heavy burthen of the State;[138]
Not for himself doth Krishna linger down
Far from his golden halls of perfect rest:
And, would his servants do their lord's behest,
Who cheerful work their work are those who serve him best.

17.

"And I must ponder and meditate
The stains of the earth to expiate,
Till my heart shall be weaned from worldly things,
And my spirit resume her native wings,
And be meet for her glorious fate.
Silent the days shall flee,
Till thou shalt welcome me
With thine own voice;
Then from all sorrow free,
Shall I, beloved, with thee
Ever rejoice."

So sang she, watching by her sister river,[139]
Morning and night,
Till Krishna came his servants to deliver,
The world's delight.

Part III.

The Omens.

18.

But the gods with envy eyed
  The ocean-city's towers:
Sadly, as a mourning bride
(Who sees her warrior husband ride
  To face the invading powers,
With all his clan in mailèd pride,)
Lays her robes of joy aside,[140]
  So Vaikuntha's [141] bowers
On the wind that softly sighed,
Mazed amid their branches wide,
  Cast their half-blown flowers;
Dew-drops dripped from all their leaves,
Like the tears of her who grieves
  For a dear and absent one;
  To their master's wave-rocked throne
Far the heavy-laden air
Bore the perfume of their prayer:

And the birds their boughs among
Ever answered song to song,—
"In vain for us the richest blossoms glow;
In vain for us the coolest breezes blow;
In vain for us the freshest fountains flow;
All is to us a dreary night,—
We lack the sun of our delight;
Krishna, thou lingerest long!"

19.

Well did he for whom they sighed
Know the fate-appointed tide;
His task he now had wholly done,
Had slain the haughty chiefs each one,
Who ruled with tyrant sway,
And hurled that bold impostor down,[142]
Who dared in Shiva's holiest town
To lead the world astray.
Fate the last and darkest page
May no more delay to show;
Seen afar by saint and sage,
Black with guilt and woe,
Looms upon the earth below
The fatal Kali age.[143]

20.

Therefore did a deepening gloom
Shadow forth the city's doom;
Therefore through her dwellings ceased
Mirth and music, song and feast;
Shrieks of woe were heard at night;
Demon shapes of lurid light,
Fiendish triumph in their eyes,
Glared from out the threatening skies,
Darkening o'er the sinking sun,
Ere the night were yet begun.
Beasts with human voice foretold
Woes and sorrows manifold;
Laughter filled her homes no more;
Wailing rose from every door;
From the frequent funeral pyres
Seemed the city girt with fires,—
Camp-fires of beleaguering hosts,
Death their king, their warriors ghosts.

21.

Through the drear dark hours of night,
Veiled in vapours chill and white,

Borne along the shrieking blast,
Troops of ghastly spectres passed.
Silent now the busy feet
From the ruin-stricken street;
Each man shunned his neighbour's face,
Fearing in his eyes to trace
Some new portent direr still,
Presaging a greater ill;
Or, with whispers thronging round,
Some a dreadful pleasure found,
Shuddering while they strained to hear
Each the other's tale of fear.
But the horror chief of all
Never from their lips did fall;
By the day and by the night
Still he haunted each man's sight;
None might from his presence 'scape;
None might tell his shapeless shape;
But they closer drew their breath,
For they felt that he was Death.

22.

In Murāri's [144] palace then
Gathered Yadu's noblest men;

Him within the cool retreat,
Sheltered from the noontide heat,
To his sons and grandsons round
Teaching wisdom's truths, they found.
When the suppliants met their view,
Knowing well the honour due
To the aged and the good,
Reverent all the warriors stood.
But, in silence pacing slow,
Garbed in all the guise of woe,
Passing by the proffered seat,
Till he bowed at Krishna's feet,—
Bowed his head and joined his hand,—
Spake the eldest of the band:

23.

"Dost not thou, O Krishna, see
All thy people's misery?
Heed'st thou not thy parents' pain,
And the cares of Ugrasen?
Have thine arrows lost their might?
Is Sudarshan shorn of light?

Is our land a loathèd spot?
Are thy mercies all forgot?
No! the city of the wave
Thou didst raise, and thou shalt save:
Thou didst frame her for thine own,
Firm upon her ocean-throne;
Safe she dwelt, secure from harm,
Man or fiend, with steel or charm;
Quenched was Krityā's [145] flaming sword;
Foiled her magic arts abhorred;
Scattered Sālav's [146] countless host;
Humbled Dwivid's [147] impious boast;
Shishupāla's brethren bold
In one rapid ruin rolled.—
Now behold a fiercer foe;
Now a greater grief we know:
Seek we our defence in vain?
Loose thy conquering shafts again!
Haste, arise, thy people free!
Hear us, son of Devakī!"

24.

He ceased his prayer, and all the train
Took up the closing words again;

But the foe of Madhu[148] sighed,
As sadly he replied,
For he knew that their hopes were vain :
"Because the children of Yadu dwelt
Securely long, and no danger felt,
Now are these trials in mercy meant,
To win them again to the way they went
In the troublous times of old ;
For now are their hearts with illusion blind,
And darkness and passion have ruled each mind,
And the veil of the world hath dimmed their eyes,
And they seek not to pass beyond the skies
To the radiance these mists enfold :
For the blessings they seek are as curses sent,
And love is revealed in a chastisement,
And the favoured of heaven rest not secure,
But those who through suffering keep them pure
The secrets of truth behold.
Now are Dwārakā's destined days fulfilled,
And the power that portions our lot hath willed
We should wander away from our pleasant home,
On the shores of the barren sea to roam,
By the guidance of fate controlled.

25.

"To Arjun, [149] Indra's warrior son,
Midmost of the royal five,
Let each entrust his child, his wife;
He shall guard them forth each one,
That so our names may yet survive,
Fresh springing into newer life.
But, ye who are men, in your war array
Attend at the northern gate:
When the sky blushes red for the seventh day,
We march to seek our fate."

PART IV.

The Abandonment of the City.

26.

There, before the city wall,
Met the Yādav warriors all.
What though in him they could but trace
The conquering hero of their race;
Though, blinded by pleasure, to them was sealed
The truth which that veil of flesh concealed,

Yet they followed Krishna still;
He might lead them at his will:
In his jewelled chariot riding,
Forth he moved, their forces guiding.

27.

Still a countless host was theirs,
As the stars or as the sand;
But heavy was each heart with cares:
Musing what doom awaits the band,
What new destruction fate prepares,
In silence strode they on.
For thought had clouded Krishna's brow;
A weary weight was Rāma's [150] plough;
And fled the light of triumph now,
On every face that shone
When erst they marched in gallant show
To cope with many a haughty foe,
False Paundrak's [151] pride to overthrow,
And tame fierce Rukmin's [152] might,-
When Rāma's club and Krishna's bow
Laid Bāna's [153] demon-armies low,
And Shiva's self was forced to know
A victor in the fight.

28.

As Indra's forces move to war,
So showed their squadrons then,
When from his kingdom in the north,
Beyond all mortal ken,
High-seated on his cloud-built car,
He leads his legions forth
With rainy shafts arrayed,
And seeks the scorching plains in aid
To trees and beasts and men.
For with the rainbow's various hue
Their banners were displayed;
Like lightning flashed the rays to view
From helmet, shield, and blade;
Like distant thunder rolled the beat
Of battle-drums, and tramp of feet
From those unnumbered crowds;
And, dusky-vast as thunder clouds,
The elephants went by;
Their tusks seemed flights of large-winged cranes,
Which, joying in the coming rains,
Soaring from Anga's [154] rice-sown plains,
Go screaming through the sky.

Came the daughters of the gods;
  Came the choosers of the slain;[155]
Floating from their blest abodes
Down the bright empyreal roads,
  They sought the battle plain;
Well they knew how Yadu's sword
Gives to each a warrior lord.

29.

But now no music stirring
  From drum or cymbal breaks;
No shaft from bow unerring
  The startled stag o'ertakes;
No squadrons lightly wheeling
  Contend in mimic fray;
To prowess past appealing,
  No minstrel tunes his lay.
On they journeyed by the ocean,
  Dark and silent as the main,
Which with long and heavy motion
  Showed the coming hurricane.

Part V.

The Massacre.

30.

Tall and strong the rushes grow
Where Prabhāsa's[156] fountains flow;
There the groves are thick and green,
And the waters glide between;
Gentle breezes all the day,
Seaward rising, drive the spray;
Branches bend with fruitage sweet;
Blossoms spring beneath the feet;
Birds of song or plumage bright
Eye and ear at once delight;
Seemed the vale from Swarga riven,
And to earth a foretaste given.[157]

31.

Footsore from the burning sand,
Rested there the weary band;
There the strife-enkindling draught,
Led by destiny, they quaffed,

Heedless of command.
  Slight the spark that roused the fire :
  Signs and taunts and words of ire
Soon the tumult fanned ;
  Towards the water's brink they pressed :
  From their bed the reeds they wrest,
Grasped with nervous hand.

32.

Alas ! the mace,[158] the fatal mace,
Bane foretold of Yadu's race !
As small as dust 'twas ground,
  Yet the fragments parted not ;
Strewn on the waters round,
  They reached the destined spot.
    Sprung from that iron seed,
    Iron became each reed ;
    Yet none whose comrades bleed
      From the fight ceased :
    Wildly with frenzied eyes
    Shout they their battle-cries ;
    Swift through the camp there flies
      Madness increased :

Fiercer descend the blows;
Wilder the slaughter grows;
All in the contest close,
  Noblest and least.

33.

How may I tell
What warriors fell
  On that ill-omened day?
For not a chief of Yadu's name,
And not a clansman less in fame,
  But joined the fatal fray.
There Prithu fell, and Bhadrasen,
And Chāru's heart-blood dyed the plain,
And mighty Durgama was slain,
  And Shruta lifeless lay.[159]

34.

There perished Jāmbavatī's son,
  Whom the Kurus[160] seized and bound,
When he Duryodhan's daughter won
  From the suitors thronged around,
Till Rāma came to his nephew's aid,
Alone in the might of his wondrous blade

(The tamer of Yamunā's waters blue);—[161]
Then their tyrannous force was stayed:
For the elephant-city his prowess knew,
When her tottering walls to the stream he drew,
And the princes hastened for peace to sue.
And freed the youth and maid.

35.

Sāmba his name, and from his side
The accursed club was born;[162]
For so the sages he defied
Had in their anger sworn
Of him, by whom of bashful bride
(In foolish thought his state to hide)
The soft attire was worn;
In recklessness of youthful pride
With mocking tale their power he tried,
And age and wisdom dared deride,
And turn to jest and scorn.

36.

There Kritavarman sank in fight,
Of counsel dark and deep;
Who aided Drona's[163] son to smite

The Pāndav camp at silent night,
And did with subtle art incite
Satrājit's death in sleep;
But soon a heavy reckoning paid
The murderer, for the tears he made
Fair Satyabhāmā [164] weep.

37.

There princely Aniruddha died
Beneath the ruthless mace,
Who in a vision viewed his bride
Of Bāna's royal race; [165]
When fairy wings did gently glide,
And with the slumberer softly hied
Where blushing she, and bashful-eyed,
Awaited his embrace,
Though bars of brass the castle bound,
And demon-warders watched around;
No tower of strength was ever found,
But Love should win his place.

38.

And, when the peacock-flag, that lay,
Its pride with dust bestained,

To him the intruder did betray
  Who o'er the Daityas reigned,
And, torn from her embrace, he lay
  With serpent fetters chained.
True-hearted to each other they
  In threats and scorn remained:
Till friendly armies did convey
The pair along their homeward way,
With bridal pomp and music gay
  And triumph unrestrained;
Though Bāna braced, their march to stay,
  The thousand arms he gained,
And all the fiends that owned his sway
  The contest fierce maintained,
And all who Shiva's rule obey,
And Shiva's self in dread array.
  To aid his votary deigned.

39.

And there too shared the common fate
Akrūra, leader wise and great,
  Of dauntless hardihood,
Who in the counsels of the state
  In chiefest reverence stood;

Who Sūrya's gift [166] in days of yore,
The wealth-bestowing jewel, wore,
  So virtue-rich there could
No evil linger on the shore,
But peace and health and golden store,
And fortune flowing more and more
  To universal good.

40.

There lay Pradyumna [167] stark and cold,
  And dimmed that gleaming sword
Which back the tide of battle rolled
  When Yadu's heroes warred;
He in whose form of angel mould
Did Ratī, queen of love, behold
  Her long-lamented lord
(In beauty pure, as when he died
By Shiva's glance of anger eyed,)
  To life and her restored.

41.

But Krishna strove their rage to quell,
  Though all his words were vain,
Until his loved Pradyumna fell;—

Then all the father's wrath did swell
  Within his maddened brain;
At once he hurled his discus fell,
  And heaped the earth with slain.
Of all the tribe that self-same morn
  Saw forth so stately wend,
(Now strewn, as lies the mellow corn
  When the reaper's labours end,
  Brother on brother, friend on friend,—
Slain by the hand that once had borne
  All dangers to defend,)
There was none living, far or near,
Save Krishna and his charioteer.

42.

Then to their lord returned no more
  The ensigns of his might;
Swift, swift, along the level shore
The steeds the car celestial bore,
Till ocean's waves with sullen roar
  Had swept them from the sight.
The mace, the disc, yet red with gore,
Well knew their earthly labours o'er,
And, herald-like, their king before
  They winged their heavenward flight.

Part VI.

The Triumph.

43.

But Balarāma sat apart,
Beneath a mango's shade,
Still brooding in his moody heart
O'er kindred strife that made
The Kurus' field a slaughter-place
For chiefs their ancient line who trace [168]
From Sūrya glory-rayed,
And Soma, god of milder face,—
And mighty kings of alien race
Who marched their troops to aid.

44.

When on a sudden there befell
A portent dread and strange to tell,
While Dāruk [169] viewed amazed;
For forth from Rāma's [170] mouth there came
A serpent vast, with eyes of flame,
And, more and more as swelled his frame,
A thousand crests he raised.

As toward the sea his course he drew,
The Nāgas [171] thronged around to view.
And snakes of every size and hue
Upon their monarch gazed;
The tide advanced his steps to greet,
And water-nymphs with twinkling feet,
And ocean-gods brought offerings meet,
And Ocean, welcoming his retreat,
With fiery radiance blazed.

45.

"Lo, Shesha! lo, the serpent king!"
The wondering Dāruk cried,
"Who girds the world with monstrous ring,
Who o'er the milky tide
Supports, with crests high towering,
Vaikuntha's [172] throne of pride,—
Whose praises gods and sages sing."
But Krishna calm replied:—
"This thou hast seen; these tidings bear
To Ugrasena's palace fair,
And tell my parents anxious there,
Of all that did betide;
Yet see thou charge them not despair,

For soon shall they through fast and prayer,
Be raised to bliss unfailing, ne'er
  Dissevered from my side.
But let the weak and young repair
To some new city 'neath the care
Of Prithā's[173] son of flowing hair,
  Arjun, my comrade tried:
So still the crown shall Vajra[174] wear,
And so the noble name we share
  Shall not have wholly died:
For Yadu's children yet shall reign
O'er peopled town and fertile plain,
Till Vishnu seek mankind again,
And purging earth of sin and pain,
  His milk-white steed[175] bestride.
But Dwārakā, her pomp is o'er,
  Her days of fate are run;
Her golden turrets never more
Shall flash their beams upon the shore
  Back to the rising sun."

46.

So Krishna charged him, as he sate
Expectant of the coming fate,

By him denounced who ne'er doth bate
  Aught of his anger fierce:
A hunter's arrow erring sped
(That fatal iron formed its head)
  His lotus foot to pierce.
'Twas so Durvāsas[176] had decreed;
And so, from fleshly trammels freed,
His soul, which all doth animate,
Reverted to its pristine state.

47.

But faintly hath my spirit striven
  With earthly lips and cold;
Oh that to me the soul were given
  Of the godlike bards of old!
Of him, ere Rāma yet was born,[177]
Of Sītā from her husband torn,
Mourning in Lankā's isle forlorn,[178]
Of Rāma's wrath, and Rāvan's scorn,
  The wondrous tale who told;
Or him who sang what kingly rite
  Did just Yudhishthir hold;
Of Arjun's deeds, and Bhīma's[179] might,

And those fair twins in valour bright,
Who stood to meet in fearful fight
The hundred brethren bold.

48.

Then would I sing, by Krishna led
How Yadu's sons arose;
Their living chariots northward sped,
Where Meru raises his awful head,
With its crown of endless snows;
Where the Siddhas[180] their flowery garlands thread,
And odours of paradise round them shed;
Where the river of heaven,[181] in crystal bed,
From the foot of Vishnu flows;
Where the Rishis[182] seven in glory shine;
And Dhruva,[183] that hermit of soul divine,
With moveless splendour glows.

49.[184]

Swift mounted the cars on their heavenward way;
By the path of the winds their journey lay,
Where the planets roll,
Bound to the pole
With chains of air, that they shall not stray.

The clouds the softest of pavements spread,
And the lightning played harmlessly round each head:
            The earth to view
            Still lessening grew,
And the wheels were sprinkled with beads of dew;
            And the chariots shone
            As they floated on,
    With rainbows of freshest hue;
Where Hemakūt [165] towers with gleaming crest,
A pillar of gold,—and on east and west
            An ocean laves
            With purple waves
    The ancient mountain's breast.

50.

Yet they turned not aside to those gardens fair,
Nor to Swarga's bowers devoid of care;
  Nor where rises Kailāsa,[186] a cone of white,
  Or Meru's waters to rest invite,
Did the conquering band repair.
For, though distant yet, to their eager sight
Vaikuntha's portals were glowing bright,
And they entered there through the flood of light
    No earthly eye can bear.

Part VII.

The Fall of Dwārakā.

51.

But, strong in their trust in Arjun's hand,
From Dwārakā wandered the weeping band;
The weak and the timid, they journeyed away,
And the home of their happiness desolate lay;
Voiceless her streets and her palaces all;
There was not an echo from wall to wall;
Silent and sad, as this earth shall be
When her elements mix in a shoreless sea;
No light above, and no life below,
Ere the winds which shall herald Creation blow,
When all is vast, and void, and deep,
And the soul of the Universe rests in sleep.[187]

52.

On her palaces many and white
The full moon shone with a ghastly light;

And the scattered clouds drove hurrying past,
Like the spirits of evil which guide the blast;
And the ocean moaned with an angry sound;
And the muttering clouds were gathering round;
And from heaven to earth the lightning rushed
In a line of flame, as though Indra crushed
And hurled to the depths his demon foes; [188]
And fiercer and fiercer the wind arose;
And nearer and nearer the thunder crashed;
And brighter and brighter the lightning flashed:
And higher and higher the waters swelled,
For the charm had departed their wrath which quelled,
And bound their free spirits in chains so long,
And now was the time to revenge the wrong;—
Then wherefore do they pause?
Why suddenly hath ceased the fierce commotion?
Have they relented of their angry will?
Or hath some hidden cause
Constrained the elements with mightier laws?
For, save the heaving bosom of the ocean,
All now is hushed and still;
And heavily, as loaded plummets drop,
The banners hang in shreds from spire and turret-
top.

53.

No sound, no stir, no sign of life ;
More dread this stillness than the roar
Of warring winds and waves before ;
They only rest to gather strength ;
And now to direr strife
The tempest sweeps along o'er Ocean's blackening length.
Winds and waves, at once they dash
On rampart, gate, and wall ;
Mid thunder crash
And lightning flash
They quake, they bend, they fall.
With burst of triumph onward sprung
The waters swelling high ;
They rushed the scattered blocks among,
And their white crests rejoicing flung
Against the murky sky.

54.

Like soldiers to sack of a citadel,
When the perilous breach they win,
By lofty street and ample square
The conquering tide poured in :

Battlement, rampart, and pinnacle,
Tower by tower, down they fell;
For the billows laid siege to each castle fair,
And stormed each humbler home:
They mined beneath, and to scale the height
They tossed their angry foam;
And they hurled vast rocks with an engine's might,
And huge blocks they tore from their laboured site,
And ground them to powder, and dragged them down,
Till there was not left of that stately town
One stone in the morning's light;
And the waves were ceasing to seethe and boil,
And the winds were calming the wild turmoil,
Victorious in the fight.

55.

Yet now at peaceful eve, as by
This ancient shrine I stand,[189]
Methinks the Ocean seems to sigh
Along the waste of sand,
Mourning the ruthless ruin wrought
In the unchanging past;

For sure so bright and holy nought
Shall mortal view in loftiest thought,
While Ocean's self shall last;
Until the fire
Of Aurva's ire,[190]
In Varun's [191] cave that sleeps,
With riven chain
Up bursts again
From out the yawning deeps;—
And, lifting proud his smoky crown
O'er forest dense, and ample down,
And awful mountain-steeps,
And fruitful field, and peopled town,
And rivers vast of old renown,
His lurid banner sweeps:
Until the vengeance is repaid,
By Brahmā's prayers so long delayed,
And all the guiltless blood which flowed
In saintly Bhrigu's pure abode
Its just requital reaps.

56.

Till earth with sea, and sea with light,
And light with thinner air unite,

In ether air be swallowed quite,
And ether in the Infinite,
  The all-pervading mind;[192]
Which whoso learns to know aright,
And soar on high with vision bright,
  Freed from illusion blind,
Will shun not pain, nor seek delight,
Nor joy in praise, nor need despite,
But good and ill as one requite,
Because not diverse in his sight
  Is he from all mankind.[193]
He will, with meditative might,
'Gainst sense a wakeful warfare fight,
Turn passion's fierce assaults to flight;
  Till, bursting links which bind
The soul to grope through error's night
From birth to birth in evil plight,
In the all-present soul his spright
  Its rest eternal find.

The Song of Kālindī.[194]

[The Hindūs divide the year into six seasons, inserting the dewy season between winter and spring, and the rains between summer and autumn.]

1.

The fresh wind blows from northern snows;
 The nights are dank with dew;
A mound of fire the Sīmal[195] glows;
 The young rice shoots anew;
In mornings cool from reedy pool
 Up springs the whistling crane;
The wild fowl fly through sunset sky;
 The sweet juice fills the cane.
Come, Krishna! from the tyrant proud
 How long shall virtue flee?
The lightning loves the evening cloud,
  And I love thee.

2.

The breeze moves slow with thick perfume
From every mango grove;
From coral tree [196] to parrot bloom [197]
The black bees questing rove;
The koïl [198] wakes the early dawn,—
He calls the spring all day;
The jasmine smiles by glade and lawn;
The lake with buds is gay.
Come, Krishna! leave Vaikuntha's [199] bower;
Do thou our refuge be;
The koïl loves the mango flower,
And I love thee.

3.

Low from the brink the waters shrink;
The deer all snuff for rain;
The panting cattle search for drink
Cracked glebe and dusty plain;
The whirlwind, like a furnace blast,
Sweeps clouds of darkening sand;
The forest flames; the beasts aghast
Plunge huddling from the land.

Come, Krishna! come, belovèd one!
  Descend and comfort me:
The lotus loves the summer sun,
    And I love thee.

4.

With dancing feet glad peafowl greet
  Bright flash and rumbling cloud;
Down channels steep red torrents sweep;
  The frogs give welcome loud;
From branch and spray hang blossoms gay;
  The wood has second birth;
No stars in skies, but lantern-flies
  Seem stars that float to earth.
Come, Krishna! in our day of gloom
  Be thou our Kalpa tree: [200]
The wild bee loves the Padma bloom,[201]
    And I love thee.

5.

The skies are bright with cloudless light,
  Like silver shells that float;
The stars and moon loom large by night;
  The lilies launch their boat;

Fair laughs the plain with ripened grain;
  With birds resounds the brake:
Along the sand white egrets stand;
  The wild fowl fill the lake.
Come, Krishna! let thy servants soon
  Thy perfect beauty see:
The water-lily loves the moon,[202]
    And I love thee.

6.

The morning mist lies close and still;
  The hoar-frost gems the lea;
The dew falls chill; the wind blows shrill;
  The leaves have left the tree;
The crops are gone; the fields are bare;
  The deer pass grazing by;
And plaintive through the twilight air
  Is heard the curlew's cry.
Come, Krishna! come, my lord, my own!
  From prison set me free:
The chakravākī [203] pines alone,
  As I for thee.

The Pilgrim's Return from Haridwāra.

[Haridwāra, Anglicé Hurdwar, is the gate of Hari, or Vishnu, that is, the place where the Ganges enters the plains through the Siwālik range.]

Bright river, bright river, how swiftly we glide
From the glow of the sunset borne on by thy tide!
No need for the rower to scare with his oar
The silence that sleeps on the wave and the shore.

The sun is fast sinking; the gold of his beam
Falls level and long on the rippleless stream;
As a saint, who hath trodden the pathway of right,
Leaves the wealth of his prayers ere he passes from sight.

All day have we shrunk from the glare of his rays,
And sought for a shelter with long wistful gaze:
But chill now and drear seems the conquering shade,
And we turn with regret to the glories that fade.

So the deeds of the holy, to angels akin,
Are not to be borne by the children of sin;
A veil 'twixt our gloom and their brightness we cast;—
Yet we cannot but mourn when for ever they're passed.

The clouds had o'ershadowed his face for a time,
As he bent from the height of his noontide sublime;
But now round the path of his triumph they spread,
And bedeck it with banners of amber and red.

And thus upon earth may the soul of the saint
In age and in trouble grow feeble and faint;
But firm at the last on his road shall he tread,
And the haloes of paradise garland his head.

No sound on the waters, no sound on the shore,
Save the tide as it breaks on the steersman's long oar,
Save the drone of the night-fly, and, hark! where yon bell
Tinkles faintly the hour of devotion to tell.

Fast deepens the twilight; the clouds, which had shone
In the smile of the sunlight, wax ghostly and wan:
Oh, what to earth's pleasures their joy can restore,
When the soul that has shared them shall share them no
more?

In the darkness they vanish; but see, from above
How their bosoms are lit by the lightning they love:
So, though purer and calmer, those joys 'twill renew
To dream that that spirit partakes of them too.

At once round the sky, from the south to the north,
The firmament's fires into living flash forth;
As a curtain of silver had half been unrolled
For a glimpse of a citadel burning with gold.

The full moon has risen majestic and still;
The messenger rays speed the heaven to fill;
Their tidings the stars with due reverence hail;
At the face of their monarch their splendours they veil.

The sunset's warm glow soon deserted our track.
As the visions of youth turn to mourning and black;
But before us how soft beams the light from the wave,
Like the calmness which whispers of peace in the grave!

The river,[204] awhile by the darkness concealed,
Bears us onward once more into vastness revealed;
But the eye of the wanderer scarcely can trace
Where Gangā flows on in her heavenly race.

So the joys which the sons of mortality bless,
Shine broad and distinct in the light of success;
But he who the secrets above us would know,
Must have watched through the shadows of trouble and woe.

As the truth which our teachers in emblems declare,
By the mystical thread the regenerate wear,—
So twice have these sin-purging waters their birth: [205]
They are born in the heaven, and born in the earth.

The pathway to heaven of Sagara's sons,
From her ice-moulded cradle how holy she runs!
But who of her glories celestial may sing,
Where unsullied she bursts from her heavenly spring?

O favoured of Shiva! 'twas only by thee
Might Sagara's sons [206] immortality see;
Other cleansing availed not for souls which were dyed
So deep in the stains of presumption and pride.

With a vow to recover the steed of their sire,
Forth sallied the brothers, transported with ire;
Six myriad princes, the earth they o'erran,
And they pierced to the regions forbidden to man.

Down, down to Pātāla, they quarried their way,
And the kingdoms unknown to the brightness of day;
The light gleamed unwonted on temples and domes,
And the jewelled abodes of the Nāgas [207] and gnomes.

The kings of the serpents, the ancient and wise,
From their centuries' slumber awoke in surprise;
They fled to their caverns the tumult to shun,
While the gold of their diadems flashed in the sun.

In vain were the threats and the vauntings of pride:
Consumed by a glance of the sage they defied,
Their ashes lay strewn on the rocks of the cave,
Awaiting the touch of the life-giving wave.

For ages on ages king Sagara's heirs
Besought their salvation with penance and prayers;
But penance and prayers were found wanting in worth,
Till Bhagīratha's merits brought Gangā to earth.

Ill brooked she to bow to a mortal's command,
But the might of devotion no will may withstand;
So, chafing in pride of her lineage high,
On the snow-covered mountains she sprang from the sky.

Down the gullies in anger she hurriedly leapt;
O'er the rocks and the boulders she scornfully swept;
In her blue waving-mantle, with lotuses crowned,
Divine in her beauty, she passed to the ground.

The fields of the villager burst into green,
Where the trace of her white twinkling footsteps was
seen;
Came the gods and the mortals her praises to sing,
As disdainful she followed the car of the king.

By plain and by forest rejoicing he drave,
Till his coursers he checked at the sepulchre-cave;
Till the feet of the goddess those ashes had pressed,
And his kinsmen had passed to the realms of the blest.—

But mark where yon lamps flicker dim on the right;
The village is near where we sojourn to-night:
Speed, rowers, speed swiftly the boat on her way,
And rest shall repay you the toils of the day.

The Moral of History.

(FROM THE VISHNU PURĀNA.)

1.

Thou hast heard me tell, Maitreya,[208] of the lords of Manu's[209] line:
Kings of wealth unbounded; heroes gifted with a soul divine;

2.

Saints who toiled with mighty penance stains of earth to expiate;
Sages who through years unnumbered strove against the stream of fate;

3.

Kings and heroes, saints and sages, famous in the days of yore;—
Thou hast heard of these, Maitreya, but their deeds are seen no more.

4.

Yet they styled themselves the masters of the ever-during
world,
By one destiny relentless to the same destruction hurled.

5.

And by time they learn not knowledge: each proclaims in
haughty tones,
"Mine is earth, the sea-encircled; mine with all her
seven zones:[210]

6.

"Mine they are, my race shall hold them:" each in turn
his heart beguiles;
At the folly of her masters, Earth with autumn-blossoms
smiles.

7.

For they think not other monarchs ruled with mightier
sway of yore,
And the sons shall fall and perish, as the fathers fell before.

8.

Kin with kin, and sires with children, strive by lust of
sway impelled,
Which the ancient kings retained not, which their fathers
have not held.

9.

Yet they love a nobler conquest, and a rule of greater
worth;
What to him, o'er self a victor, is the ocean-girdled earth?

10.

Foolish were the kings who boasted, "Earth is mine,
mankind my slaves:"
Time, more mighty, hath o'ercome them; silent sleep they
in their graves.

11.

Prithu,[211] o'er his foes triumphant, reigned with universal
sway:
Whirled before the blast of time, like Sīmal-down,[212] he
passed away.

12.

He who once was Kārtavīrya[213] through all lands a victor
went:
Now the subject of a legend, and a theme for argument.

13.

Raghu's[214] sons their rule extended to the wide world's
utmost zone,—
By the frown of the Destroyer in a moment overthrown.

14.

Lived they then, these potent chieftains? where are now
the strong and brave?
Nought know we; their traces vanish, as the foam upon
the wave.

15.

When they listen to these annals, truest wisdom who have
won,
Fades ambition at the hearing as the snow before the
sun.

16.

Wife and children—wealth—dominion,—deeming nought
on earth thine own,
Fix thy heart on lasting riches stored around the Eternal
Throne.

The Force of Nature.

A crow flew over the hermitage;
He dropped a mouse at the feet of the sage.

The sage took up the helpless thing,
And washed its wounds in the holy spring.

With a gentle hand he bore it away,
And tended its hurts through many a day.

With a father's love he loved it well:
He made it a damsel by might of spell.

She grew in beauty, she grew in grace,—
She held in his bosom a daughter's place.

"My daughter is meet for a husband now:
To whom wilt thou plight thy marriage vow?"

"Happy our life in the woodland here:
Why should I leave my father dear?"

"The father sinneth a sin," he said,
"Who sees not his child in honour wed."

"If I must leave my maiden state,
The strongest of beings I choose for mate."

They went to the sun in his noonday height:
"Sure none can equal thy glorious might?"

"How can he claim that matchless praise,
When every cloud can hide his rays?"

They went to the cloud rolling black from the west:
"O thunder-voiced, is thy strength the best?"

"How is he strongest, when to and fro
As the wind may list he is forced to go?"

They went to the wind that was shouting free:
"Unwearied of wing, is the strength with thee?"

"How can he make so proud a claim,
When the hill is able his force to tame?"

They went to the hill in his snowy length:
"O pillar of earth, is thine the strength?"

"How can he boast such rank to fill,
When the little brown mouse bores his roots as he will?"

They went to the mouse: "Enough," said she,
"The little brown mouse my lord shall be."

"The force of nature exceeds my lore!"
He made the damsel a mouse once more.

To the Kalkī Tree.

[The kalki tree (Plumienia) is planted by the Muhammadans of India over graves. Its branches are short and thick, and do not taper at all. They are often entirely leafless; but it is rarely, if ever, out of blossom. Its flowers are white, with a yellow centre,—in fragrance, as in appearance, somewhat resembling orange blossom. They are very fleshy, and thus retain their freshness long after they fall.]

WELL have our fathers done,
Tree of the silent one;
Still in thy praise shall the story be said;
Well did they, choosing thee
First of the wood to be
Watcher and guard of the graves of the dead.

Others are fairer trees,
Waving along the breeze,
Bending with mourners the wan weeping head;
Rough and uncouth thy form,
Steadfast before the storm,
Pointing to heaven from the graves of the dead.

Others have brighter hue,
Heaven's own stainless blue,
Purity's white, and affection's deep red;
Thou, with thy blossoms pale,
Scentest the evening gale,
Hallowing with incense the graves of the dead.

Others a little while
Welcome our joyous smile,
Fainting and weary ere summer is fled;
Thou, through the wintry day,
Dost the old care repay,
Faithful and true by the graves of the dead.

Others have shadowed screen,
Where the sweet birds, unseen,
Sing the wild notes on the waving leaves read,
Thou, from thy leafless bough,
Puttest forth flowers enow,
Smiling through grief o'er the graves of the dead.

Others their treasures cast
After the bloom is past,—

Withered and scentless the gifts that they shed;
  Thou, while thou flourishest,
  Givest thy first and best,
Strewing thy buds o'er the graves of the dead.

  Therefore thy name we praise,
  As in the former days
When on the tombs thy first offerings were spread;
  Fresh flowers day by day
  Thou shalt unwearied lay,
Sentinel sure at the graves of the dead.

MISCELLANEOUS BALLADS.

Hymn of Spartan Matrons.

1.

By the adoration paid thee
  In thy great Ephesian fane;
By the sacrifices made thee
  Far beyond the Tauric main; [215]

2.

Where thou sav'dst the Argolic maiden [216]
  From her father's fatal knife,
That Orestes, sorrow-laden,
  She might bring again to life;

3.

Hear us, hear us! we adore thee
  By thy threefold name divine;
Hear us, as we bow before thee,
  Luna, Cynthia, Proserpine!

4.

Who, with silver-footed horses,
Luna! thou of gentle light!
Guid'st the planets' wandering courses,
Rulest o'er the orbs of night;

5.

Cynthia! with thy darts uprousing—
Tall amidst thy buskined maids—
Boar or stag, the thickets browsing,
In the deep Arcadian glades;

6.

Proserpine! o'er Hades swaying,
Consort of thine uncle's throne,
Who, in Enna's meadows playing,
Saw and seized thee for his own.

7.

By thy dear Endymion's beauty; [217]
By thy Virbius,[218] ever found
Faithful to the path of duty;
By Adonis' [219] yearly wound;

8.

Let the kings, from Jove descended,
In the unwalled city bred,
Conquer now, by thee defended,
Who before thy shrine have bled.

9.

But let fall as fell Actæon,—
As Pirithous,[220]—so fall they,
Argive false, or Mantinean,
Who shall dare to bar their way.

10.

Let no sight of evil omen
Fill our hearts with sad mistrust:
Let us live to see our foemen
Humbled lowly in the dust.

11.

But if, our entreaties spurning,
Thou refusest victory;
Even then, in anger turning,
Grant our sons may bravely die.

12.

Or if, woe on woe repeated,
  (Ne'er saw Sparta such a day),—
If our troops return defeated,
  And their shields be cast away,—

13.

One request thou'lt not withhold us;
  With thy kind and gentle dart,
Ere the fatal news be told us,
  Smite, O smite us, to the heart! [221]

14.

Hear us, hear us! we implore thee
  By thy threefold name divine;
Hear us, as we bow before thee,
  Luna, Cynthia, Proserpine!

Lament of the Thebans on the Death of Epaminondas.

ARGUMENT.

[The minstrel (v. 1) laments the curse which attends the city of Thebes (v. 24) from the time of Œdipus, and (v. 42) its latest effect in the loss, with the death of Epaminondas, of the pre-eminence which she had acquired under his direction. He (v. 76) mourns over the death of the hero in a foreign land, but (v. 94) triumphs in his exploits of humbling Sparta and (v. 106) delivering Messene. He (v. 126) prophesies for him a place with the guardian deities of Theban birth, Bacchus, Hercules, and the Dioscuri; and, to show the superhuman origin of the Sparti, from whom Epaminondas descended, he (v. 152) relates the legend of Cadmus and the dragon's teeth. To raise the subject of his song to Olympus, he (v. 260) invokes the aid of Bacchus and (v. 336) Hercules, by the favour they have bestowed on mortals, even some who were not of their native city; and he (v. 370) foretells the prosperity of the land, with such a patron in the courts of Olympus.]

1.

Woe to the seven-gated walls,
Which rose to the sound of song! [222]
And woe to our father Cadmus' halls!
For the curse endureth long.

2.

O Ate,[223] goddess who alone
Ne'er standest by the Olympian throne;
Banished from that blessed seat,
Thou watchest for the sinner's feet.
With thy calm blue eyes pursuing
The path that leads to his undoing;
As the waves which evermore
Wash Crissæa's cursed shore,[224]
Calm and blue and pitiless,
Never wearying, onward press.

3.

All the gods who reign above
Sacrifice and prayer may move;
All who hold the realms below
Grace and mercy sometimes show:
To thee alone
With heart of stone
Is soft compassion never known;
Nought can lure thee from the track,
Nought avails to turn thee back.

4.

Thou didst doom the banished king [225]
To his darksome wandering;
Thine were all the woes that came
On the heirs of guilt and shame;
Wretched end to wretched life
Of his hapless mother-wife.
Seven princes sought our shore,—
Sought it to return no more;
Raging fell fraternal hate
  Brother slew by brother's hand;
And the sister's love as great
  Disobeyed the stern command.
Not thus, O Ate, goddess dread,
  Wouldst thou withdraw thy hand,
Still hovering o'er the sinner's head,
  Still hovering o'er the fated land.
Nor frequent punishment nor length of time
Could wash away the wretched monarch's crime.

5.

We have known in days gone by
  Many a dark and evil hour;
We have seen through treachery
  Our city in a stranger's power: [226]

Till a morning bright and cheering
  Rose above the eastern sea;
Greece, the yoke of tyrants fearing,
  Called on us, and she was free.
Now alas! our glory fades,
  Quenched in sudden night too soon;
Darkest seem those evening shades
  Which succeed the brightest noon.
When the sun hath veiled his splendour,
  Can the stars the day retain?
Where obtain we a defender,
  Fit successor of the slain?

6.

Queen of Bœotia, wake and weep!
Rouse thee from sleep!
The eye that guarded thee shall never watch again;
  The cypress branches wave
  Above the lonely grave
Where sleeps thy bravest son on Mantinea's plain.

7.

Queen of Bœotia, wake!
Doff the diadem from thy brow;
  Hear the dying words he spake,—
"Thebes hath none to lead her now."

8.

Queen of Bœotia, wake and weep!
How shalt thou longer keep
Thy royal station 'midst the lands of Greece?
They who freed thee from the yoke,
Who the pride of Sparta broke,
Who bade Messene's thraldom cease.
All, all are sunk in endless sleep!
Queen of Bœotia, wake and weep!

9.

He resteth not the tomb within
Where side by side his fathers lie:
Far from country and from kin
The warrior drew his parting sigh;
Stranger hands his body dressed
In its white funereal vest,
And twined around his pallid brow the wreath;
Strangers raised the mourning cries,
And bade the stone sepulchral rise
To tell a Theban hero slept beneath.

10.

When again the circling hours
  Bring the ne'er forgotten day,
Who shall strew his grave with flowers,
  And guard the pillar from decay?
Who with gifts, the manes' due,
  Shall reverence the hallowed ground?
Who shall wreathe the garlands new
  His dragon monument around?[227]

11.

By Corinthus, Queen of Waters,
  To the Apian land[228] he came;
Long shall Lacedæmon's daughters
  Dread Epaminondas' name.
She, who, by her sons defended,
  Trusted not in walls of stone,[229]
Saw her long dominion ended,
  All at Leuctra overthrown.
She, who boasted ne'er invader
  Dared to tread her haughty coasts,
Trembling stood with none to aid her,
  Taunted by the Theban hosts.

12.

See! a great and ancient nation
Calls on Thebes for liberation,
Calls on Thebes,—nor calls in vain;
Broken now the tyrant's chain.
Welcome back the warrior-ghosts,
  Greet Messene's hero-shades,[230]
Wandering long on stranger coasts,
  Or in satyr-haunted glades,
Or gazing from their mountain caves,
  Where far beneath their country lay,
Or sighing to the mournful waves
  In the Cyparissian bay.[231]

13.

See! they come, a guardian band,
  To the soil they loved so well;
They who left their native land
  When strong Ithome[232] fell.
They who unyielding died
  On Ira's[233] leaguered hill,
When the fig-tree drank beside
  Dark Neda's fatal rill.

14.

Hero! though thou liest slain
On the Mantinean plain,
Still thy glorious works remain
To tell thou hast not lived in vain.
Thou shalt hold an equal place
With the guardians of our land;
Thou shalt shield the Æolic race[234]
From the strong oppressor's hand;
From the slavish traitor's snares,
From the might of hostile powers,
Thou, invoked by Theban prayers,
Still shalt save Cadmea's[235] towers.

15.

For thou art not the first
By Theban mother nursed,
Who reached at length the Olympian brazen floor;
In trials past on earth
They whilome proved their worth;
Now in the golden halls they dwell for evermore.
Ours is the king of mirth,
Of the line of Cadmus sprung,
Born in the wondrous birth,
Iacchus[236] ever young;

Ours is the god who strove
  With the labours[237] long abiding;
And ours the sons of Jove,
  Upon milk-white coursers riding.[238]

16.

'Twas not from a human stock
  That thy wondrous lineage sprung;
'Twas not from the Delphian rock
  By old Deucalion[239] flung;
But 'twas from the Serpent's might,
  Of more than earthly mould,—
Fit emblem of the Infinite,
  With his backward wreathèd fold.[240]

17.

When the wearied stranger-band,
  By the sacred heifer led,[241]
Reached at length the promised land,
  And marked the sign accomplishèd,
Then shouts of gladness rose
  From all the anxious throng;
They had passed through troubles and woes,
  And had closed their wanderings long:

Now they spoke of rest and home,
Rushing on with hasty feet,
To raise an altar meet
For the king of the Pythian dome.

18.

But beneath a branching elm
The royal exile lay;
He looked on his new-found realm,
Yet his thoughts were far away.
He thought of his sister's loss;
He thought of his father's ire;
And he thought of the sea which he might not cross,
Nor breathe the air of Tyre.
He looked on the waters glancing
Through meadow and fertile lea,
But he thought of the blue waves dancing
On Sidon's subject sea.
He looked on the waving flowers,
And the pine trees dark and tall,
But he thought of the bannered towers
Of Sidon's guarded wall.

He looked on the cattle grazing
  Along Ismenus'[242] shore,
Or in sleepy wonder gazing
  On man unseen before:
But he thought of the varied throng,
  Hastening with eager feet;
Of the merchants the wealthy marts among,
  And the crowd in the busy street.

19.

Wanderers, talk ye of rest and ease?
  Apollo doth not hear.
Why do ye seek yon gloomy trees,
  Nor dream that fate is near?
Ye claim of your chief the rites of the grave,
  And vengeance sweet in death;
Ye lie in the dragon's cave,
  Destroyed by his baleful breath.
Cadmus, strong in the favour of Jove,
Fearlessly enters the fatal grove;
    The fight is done,
    And the victory won,
And he stands alone in a lonely land beneath the
  setting sun.

20.

A king without a people! a land with none to dwell!
Are these the gorgeous visions the oracles foretell,
Of princes great and glorious who trace their birth from thee?
Of neighbour cities subject,—a people brave and free?
All this shall be, and more than this; nor disbelieve, nor doubt;
The ways of the gods are wonderful, and who shall search them out?
All shall be that hath been said,
All shall be accomplishèd:
The god disclosed the way, who speaketh not in vain.
Reeking still with Tyrian gore.
Forth the dreadful fangs he tore.
And laid beneath the plain.

21.

As the clouds of thunder part,
When the god with forky dart
Smites the man of impious heart,
See the field its clods uprear!
Shield and sword and glancing spear,
Plumes of armèd men appear.

Forth they rose of race divine,
Parents of the Spartian line :[243]
  They knew not the cry
  Of infancy,
Nor a parent's fostering care :
  They plied not the flame
  Their weapons to frame
In the ruddy furnace glare :
  They sought not for gain
  In labour and pain.
Nor pleaded a father's fame :
  But they started to life
  Arrayed for the strife.
And their own right hands were their claim.

22.

By the gods with favour eyed,
  And to Venus' daughter[244] wed.
In his children and his bride
  Blest the life that Cadmus led ;
Till all-controlling fate
  Came upon them from above :
One died by Juno's hate,
  And the son of Saturn's love ;[245]

Inflamed by frenzy, one
Destroyed her royal son; [246]
And one (her offspring dead,
By him who gave them birth in madness slain,)
Across the white Megarian plain
In hasty terror fled,—
Then leaping from the rocky height she plunged beneath the main; [247]
While from Juno, ne'er relenting, on the hated town,
And on Laius' [248] royal race a greater evil fell;
Till he, the nameless stranger, to whom we gave the crown,
Unwitting wrought the baleful deed that tongue may never tell.

23.

What god shall we implore
Our hero to restore,
And from Elysian shades bring back to light of day?
Best is he of Theban birth,
He who overran the earth,
Bringing all the sons of men beneath his peaceful sway. [249]

24.

He saw the star-crowned maid of Crete,[250]
With strained eyes watching the traitor fleet;
Sadly she thought on her cheerless lot,
On gratitude, pity and love forgot,—
Murmuring over the broken vows
Sworn so oft by her faithless spouse.

25.

For him the secret clue she wrought,
  And her royal state forsook;
  No thought of her father's love she took,
Of her native land no thought:
For him she forgot the vengeance due
  To a murdered brother's ghost,
And sailed away o'er the waters blue
  From the hundred-citied coast.

26.

Evil upon thy ships alight!
Where are the sails that should be white?
Nemesis vieweth thy weeping bride;
Weep thou the tears of a parricide!

27.

Her hast thou from her kingdom taken,
And left upon a desert strand;
But thou shalt die by all forsaken,[251]
An exile from thy native land.
Thou a faithless spouse shalt love,
And doom a guiltless son to die;[252]
Thy mother through thy crime shall prove
A wearisome captivity.[253]

28.

Weep no more beside the sea!
Ariadne, weep no more!
He is at hand to comfort thee,
Whom all mankind adore;
Worthy of thy love is he,—
Let the false and perjured flee!

29.

Now from every brake there swarm
Creatures of fantastic form;
Satyrs, Fauns, and Nymphs are seen;
On they come, a motley rout;
All with song and mirthful shout
Hail their goddess and their queen.

30.

But woe to those who spurn
The thyrsus-bearing crew!
Upon themselves return
The evils they would do.
'Twas thus that Pentheus died,[254]
And thus the lord of Thrace,[255]
Who down Nyscion's side
The frantic flight did chase.

31.

But we at seasons meet
Go forth the god to greet,
On dark Cithæron's hill[256] to join the Mænad rout;
To hail Thyone's[257] son,
With loosened locks we run,
Whilst all the caverned rocks re-echo to our shout.

32.

On nimble feet dancing,
With torches wild glancing,
We call on the godhead our bosoms to fill;
On his tiger-drawn car,
See! he comes from afar,
And the hearts of the nations bow down to his will.

33.

Wave the torches, wave them higher;
  Ivy-crowned, the thyrsus wave;
He his followers shall inspire,—
  He the vine to mortals gave.
"Evœ Bacche!" hear us cry;
  Hear the Thebans, Theban-born;
Raise our hero to the sky;
  Leave us, leave us not forlorn.
Two of Cadmus' line descended
  Thou hast raised above the earth;
Her who thine infancy attended,—[258]
  Her who perished at thy birth.[259]

34.

Call we on him, the Theban pride,
  From chaste Alcmena born,
By whom the shaggy hide,
  The Nemean spoil, is worn;[260]
In the dangers oft repeated,
  He went, and fought, and overcame:
Ne'er dejected, ne'er defeated,—
  Ever honoured be his name!

35.

By that lake whose waters flow
Ninefold round the realms of woe,
Darkling down the deep descent,
Girt by secret snares he went ;
And, 'midst horrors confident,
  From the cave of gloomy hue,
By the aid which Pallas sent,
  Forth the dog of Hades drew.[261]
Soon the spell-bound chain he rent,
  And (by all the gods abhorred)
From the rock of punishment
  Freed Thessalia's impious lord,[262]
Though he dared to seek as bride
Her who sits by Pluto's side.

36.

To the sacrilegious stranger
  Such the pity he could show ;
Thus could he, despising danger,
  Save him from deservèd woe.
Never to his country's prayer
  Deaf shall he remain ;
The blameless chief to upper air
  He shall lead again.

Distant climes he treads no longer,
Vassal to another's will;[263]
More exalted now and stronger,
He shall hear his votaries still.

37.

Then, Epaminondas, thou
In the blissful seats shall reign;
From Olympus' lofty brow
Thou shalt guard the Hellenic plain.
Mindful of thine earthly station,
Bring to reconciliation
Juno, and whoe'er from high
Looks on Thebes with evil eye.

38.

When invading hosts surround us,
And their numerous bands confound us,
Thou shalt turn their ranks to flight,
And our broken line unite:
When the toiling phalanx[264] tire,
Thou shalt hope and strength inspire;
And unseen the squadrons lead,
Mounted on immortal steed;

Or teach the Sacred Band[265] to die,—
Those who know not how to fly.

39.

From folly and from treachery
Thou shalt keep our councils free:
But the wisdom of the foe
Turn to scorning and to woe:
Thou shalt shield each Theban's life,
Save the land from civil strife,
Still preserve thy country free,
And thy people worthy thee.

To Winter.

Why, Winter, draw'st thou near
To close the flying year,
That all too quickly guides his eager steed,
(Our duties left undone,)
And bid'st another sun
Move on from cold to heat, and back to cold recede?

Why leave thy gloomy reign
Beyond the frozen main,
Where murky clouds brood darkening o'er thy head:
Where heaven's artillery
Is silent in the sky,
In presence of thy might entranced with awful dread?

Vast icebergs round thee spread
Encanopy thine head,

Which ne'er have felt the sun-ray from afar:
While emerald and sapphire
Vie with the ruby's fire,
From all their myriad points shot back irregular.

Yet genial light of day,
Or warmth of torches' ray,
Ne'er shone reflected through those chambers high;
But meteors dim and drear
Came circling round them near,
And gleams of sprites that still wage combat in the sky.

There stands thine ancient throne
In islands never known,
For aye unvisited by human sight;
Thou reignest there sublime,
Unmoved by age or time,
Or lapse of seasons past, or change from day to night.

Crests of the mountain-wave!
O'er you his chariot drave
With ice-wheels gleaming in the sunbeam cold;
And stilled was every storm
When that mysterious form
Above their foam-crowned tops his magic wand did hold.

The north winds bleak and chill
Swept o'er the surface still,
That to their king they might a shade afford;
Yet locked in chains of rest
Remained the ocean's breast:
Within its bosom they touched no responsive chord.

Their yellow leaves the trees
Flung on the passing breeze,
When he did move beneath with noiseless tread;
And Spring and gentle May
Fled southward far away,
Till from the strengthened sun his train had homeward sped.

The rivers struck with awe
Grew silent as they saw,
And ceased their murmurs deep, unchecked before;
The wondrous shape to greet,
They spread before his feet
A path of firmest ice that stretched from shore to shore.

But we will bar the door
And heap on faggots more,

Soon as his lingering step without we know ;
Till at the threshold down
He cast his icy crown,
And wreathe his aged brows with holly's cheerful glow.

Then is he welcome here,
To hail the new-born year
With songs of thankfulness and sober mirth :
And bid the Christmas bell
Its God-sent tidings tell
Of mercy gentle-eyed come down to dwell on earth.

The Silent Land.

> Into the Silent Land,
> Ah! who shall lead us thither?
>
> LONGFELLOW.

THEY are gone to the Silent Land,
Yet deem not they cease to hear us;
An ever-present band,
Their spirits are watching near us.

We wend not our way alone,
For they speak with a silent voice;
They soften the heart of stone,
And they make the sad rejoice.

Oft in our lonely hours
Our heart their tale receives;
It is rung from the bells of flowers;
It is sighed by the rustling leaves:

It is murmured by rushing streams:
It is traced by the insect's flight;
It is written in glad sunbeams,
And the stars of the purple night:

It is chanted by warbling birds;
It is borne on the evening breeze:
And it joins with the ceaseless words
That go up from the solemn seas.

In our season of joy and pride,
In the flush of our manhood's powers,
In life's gay summer-tide,
When the thorns are hid by flowers:

With a whisper soft and sad
They breathe in memory's ear,
Lest our souls should be over-glad,
And we dream that our home is here.

In the hour of grief and shame,
When we feel indeed alone,
Have we not heard our name
In a well-remembered tone?

Hath it not made us strong
  To battle with life anew,
Retracing our steps of wrong,
  And striving toward the true?

But a gentler voice have they
  In our night of pain and sorrow;
They tell us how bright the day,
  And they point to a brighter morrow.

When we seek for a hand to stay,
  And we sigh for a heart to love us,
They roll the clouds away,
  And point to the stars above us.—

They are gone to the Silent Land,
  Yet their spirits are watching near us;
And, with trouble on either hand,
  They whisper hope to cheer us.

Why should we wish them back
  On this sea of trouble and pain?
They have found a shorter track
  The haven of rest to gain:

No longer in doubt to roam,
  To struggle, and fall, and faint,—
They have passed to a fairer home
  No finger of man can paint.

They have a nobler task,
  On their errands of love to fly :—
Oh ! let us rather ask
  To be written with them on high.

The Two Angels.

FROM THE "PARABLES OF KRUMMACHER."

Two angels wandered through the world
  At the holy eventide;
Awhile their noiseless wings they furled
  On a purple mountain side.

The sounds of simple merriment
  Showed where the hamlets lay:
Homeward the lagging oxen went
  After the weary day.

Alike in love, alike in grace,
  The brother spirits seemed,
But in the younger's eyes a trace
  Of sadder beauty gleamed.

Slowly and silently the sun
  From the hill-tops withdrew;
Slowly the stars looked one by one
  Forth from the deepening blue.

Behind the tall dark firs aloft
  Flushing with firefly glows,
The moon came up in splendour soft:—
  The elder angel rose,

And on the air which from the west
  Adown the valley passed,
From every soothing herb expressed,
  A gentle influence cast.

"Blest is our ministry," he said;
  "Since pain and grief began,
The path our Master trod we tread,
  In working love to man."

Sadly the younger spirit sighed,
  And a tear to his eyelids came;
"Happy art thou, and far and wide
  Do mortals love thy name.

"The sick man rests his trembling head;
The mourners cease to weep;
And, when they waken comforted,
They bless the gifts of Sleep.

"But me—their looks are pale with dread,
If one should breathe my name."
"Brother, take heart," he answerèd:
"Is not our lot the same?

"Man fears the night in childish heart;
But, when he wakeneth,
Will he not know thee as thou art,
And bless the gifts of Death?"

The Three Wells.

Far, far up the mountain,
  Lies the holy well,
Near the lonely beacon,
  Near the ruined cell.

Steep the path and toilsome
  Toward the mountain-crest;
Sweet, O weary climber,
  By the well to rest.

Hence, though wide the eye-range,
  Nought of man is seen;
Rock and heather upward,—
  Downward woodland green.

Village, field and pasture
  Next the woodland lie;
But the sounds of labour
  Cannot reach so high.

On the rugged pathway
  Few the steps that fare;
Scarce a distant sheep-bell
  Tinkles up the air.

But the hawk lies floating
  In the lonely sky;
From between the boulders
  Comes the plover's cry.

By the well no flowers
  Lift their spikes of red;
O'er the well no willow
  Hangs its graceful head:

Only, where the stone cross
  Worn with rains you see,
Close behind is planted
  One wild holly tree.

Yellow with the lichen
  Is the cross of stone;
But the rains which wear it
  Have not overthrown.

Fierce the winds of autumn
  Sweep across the fell,
Yet they raise no ripple
  On the holy well:

For it lies so safely,
  Sheltered by the hill,
That it keeps its surface
  Ever calm and still.

Dark and deep those waters;
  Through them can the eye
No white pebbles glancing
  In the sun descry:

Thus they serve as mirror
  To the sky alone,—
Only to the heavens,
  And the cross of stone.

Not in sultry August
  Do they fail or shrink,
Nor in wet November
  Overflow the brink:

Cool in heats of summer,—
  Clear in autumn rain,—
Through the frosts of winter
  Free from icy chain;

For their source is hidden
  Far beneath the rock,
Safe from season changes,
  As from tempest shock.

In the bygone ages,
  Once a saint, they say,
On the well that cheered him
  Did his blessing lay.

Wherefore, they who drink there
  Wondrous visions know,—
Thoughts of peace which reach not
  To the earth below.

In the clear cold starlight,
  As they watch from sleep,
They discern, though dimly,
  Counsels vast and deep,—

That eternal purpose
  Darkly understood,
All the skein of evil
  Weaving into good.

Thus their souls are lifted
  Up from mortal clay,
Till the hymns of angels
  Meet them on their way;

Who, while earthward hastening,
  In their songs rejoice
That on them has fallen
  The All-gracious choice,—

Speeding them on errands
  Which they love the best,
Charged with help and mercy
  At their Lord's behest.

Then, with mighty throbbings
  From its source above,
Beats the electric current,—
  Stream whose name is love,—

Down that chain most subtle,—
  Down those links which bind
Man with all his brothers,
  Man with angel-kind.

So they journey homeward
  To the pleasant land,
Serving, striving, aiding,
  One in heart and hand:

Stronger for the weaker
  Lingering on the way,—
Slow, yet ever mounting
  Toward the perfect day;

Treading, though but feebly,
  Where their Master trod;—
All the sons of Adam,—
  All the sons of God.

Of their nightly visions
  Such the tales they tell:
Wondrous are the virtues
  Of the holy well.

Deep within the woodland,—
  Where the shadows rest,—
Where the thickest beeches
  Hide the throstle's nest,—

Where the weeds have woven
  Such a tangled green,
Scarce the busy coneys
  Find a way between,—

Where the untrodden pathway
  Hardly leaves a trace,—
Open to the sunlight
  Lies a little space.

There a rock grey-lichened
  Breaks the hill's smooth side,
But the ferns and flowers
  All its sternness hide.

From above a rowan
  Her sweet arms doth fling,
Bending to her shadow
  In the fairy spring.

Bubbling, gushing, sparkling,
  Through the silver sand,
Pausing now,—then leaping
  As with broken band,—

Like a petted beauty
  Wilful of her will,
Forth the waters gambol
  Down the sloping hill;

Dashing, till they shower
  From the old oak's bough;
Calm, and gently lulling
  Rush and marsh-flower, now;

Green above their mosses;
  Sparkling next with foam;
Eddying, loth to wander
  From their lovely home;

Warbling o'er their pebbles
  One sweet changeless tone;
Rolling mimic thunder
  Through the heaped-up stone;

Down the rocky channel,
  'Neath the o'erarching green,
Joyously they vanish
  Towards the vale unseen.

There the earliest snowdrops
  Brave the wintry skies;
There the sweetest odours
  From the violets rise;

There the ring-dove's love-notes
  Are most frequent heard;
There the ripest berries
  Draw the wintering bird.

For that spring the fairies
  Charmed with spells of power,
Giving changeful beauty
  With the changing hour.

So, who tastes its waters,
  When the moon is high,—
When the new-leaved branches
  Cross athwart the sky,—

When the lilies faintly
  Catch the silver beams,—
When the wind-flowers whisper,—
  When the primrose dreams,—

When the lavish season,
  Like a spendthrift son,
Wastes its wealth of blossoms
  Ere the spring is done,—

Straight his sight is strengthened,
  Gifted to behold
Hidden life where Nature
  Seems most dark and cold.

From the blossoms shyly
  Peers the flower-sprite;
O'er the fountain hover
  Sylphs in rainbow flight;

Nymphs of rock and river
  Past the beeches glide,
Mourning in their beauty
  For the soul denied.

See with emerald lustre
  Rise the fairy ring;
Gaily move the dancers,
  Circling round their king;

Bright the flowery garments,—
  Bright the jewels' sheen,—
Bright the crown of dew-drops,
  Meet for elfin queen.

From above, the Troll-king
  Peers in sullen thought,
With his golden armlets,
  In the hill-cave wrought.

Lo! the vista lengthens;
  Glades are opening wide;
Down the mossy alleys
  Knight and lady ride.

Lo! enchanted towers
  In the distance rise;
Fiend and giant guard them,
  With their priceless prize.

Though the path be painful,
  Champion, do not quail;
Over all unholy
  Love and Faith prevail.—

Thus, like clouds of summer,
  Like a wizard's glass,
O'er the charmèd fountain
  Love and Beauty pass.

All that fancy pictures,
  All that poets dream,
Mingle in the visions
  By the fairy stream.

Just above the village
  Runs the winding lane,
Midst the fields of clover,
  And the springing grain.

There the ploughman's horses
  Pass with shamble slow,
And the cows to milking,
  Lowing as they go.

Overhead the hawthorns
  Stretch above the lane,
Rifling ears in harvest
  From the loaded wain.

Down the sloping hedge-bank,
  Starred with celandine,—
Where the glow-worms softly
  Through the bracken shine,—

Where the primrose-clusters
  Make the April gay,—
Gushes out the brooklet
  Where the children play.

Clear and fresh its water,
  All the country knows;
Many a cottage-pitcher
  Takes it as it flows;

Many a sheep-boy, plodding
  Through the dusty glare,
Throws its sparkling crystal
  On his yellow hair.

From the mossy stone-trough,
  Bubbling o'er the brink,
Where the weary cattle
  Stoop their heads to drink,—

By the fragrant hedgerow
  Breathing of the May,—
Onward to the village
  Runs its busy way.

By the cottage gardens,
  Heard, but scarcely seen,—
By the wickets standing
  On the village green,—

By the churchyard yew-tree.
  And the low grey tower,
And the bridge,—it hastens,
  Widening every hour.

Watering quiet orchards
  Bright with daffodils,—
Gathering strength from union
  With its neighbour rills,—

Working now in earnest
  For the merry mill,—
Now through level cornfields
  Winding soft and still,—

By the alder thickets
  Clustered on its edge,—
Washing with its ripple
  Willow-herb and sedge,—

Seeking the long river
  By the pollard-tree,—
On it bears its tidings
  To the expectant sea.

Who hath strength for climbing
  Up the toilsome hill?
Who hath time to wander
  By the woodland rill?

Could we learn the secrets
  Of the caves below,
From the self-same sources
  All their waters flow:

One the rains of heaven;
  One the nightly dew;
One the rocky cistern,
  Old, yet ever new.

He whose eyes are opened,
  Finds no need to roam
From the household waters
  Nearest to his home.

Psalm ii.

WHY do the heathen rage, and the people imagine a
vain thing?
Kings of the earth stand up, and rulers take counsel
together,—
Stand against the Lord, and take counsel against His
Anointed.
Cast we away their cords, and their bands let us break
them asunder.
He shall laugh them to scorn, the Lord that dwelleth
in heaven;
Then shall He speak in his wrath, and vex them in heavy
displeasure.
Yet have I set My King on the hill of My holiness,
Zion.
I will declare the decree, the word which Jehovah hath
spoken,—
Thou art My Son, Mine Own, Whom I this day have
begotten.

Ask of Me, and I shall give Thee the heathen to be
Thy possession;
Seek, and the uttermost parts of the earth shall be
Thine to inherit.
Thou shalt break them with iron, like potters' vessels in
pieces.
Therefore, be wise, O ye kings: ye judges of earth, be
instructed;
Serve the Lord with fear, and rejoice with trembling
before Him.
Kiss the Son, even now, lest, when He be angry, ye
perish;
Lest ye fall from the way, if His wrath but a little be
kindled.
Blessed shall all they be that put their trust in His
mercy.

Translation from Goethe.

ON every mountain brow
Is rest;
Scarce on the woodland crest
Hearest thou
Faint whispering;
The birds are all hushed on the tree.
Wait;—time will bring
Rest, even for thee.

Sic Vita.

Part I.

"This also is vanity and vexation of spirit."

All things are vain
  We pursue from our birth;
Trouble and pain
  Are born of the earth.

A numerous band,
  Whom distance shall thin,
Linked hand in hand,
  We our journey begin.

Fresh is the morning,
  And pleasant the scene;
Roses adorning
  The dew-spangled green:

Birds hover singing
  To greet the glad beams;
Bright insects are winging
  O'er murmuring streams.

Blossoms must die,
  And fondlings must perish;
That soonest shall fly
  Which dearest we cherish.

Sad are the gay,
  And joy turns to sorrow;
Too short is the day
  To prepare for the morrow.

Steep is the mountain,
  And sultry the day;
Never a fountain
  Our thirst to allay.

The fruits of the ground
  Are bitter to taste;
And for roses are found
  The rank herbs of the waste.

The skies that had flattered
  Are angry and red;
Our comrades are scattered,
  And pleasure is dead.

Some sadly weeping
  Have hopelessly strayed;
Some sought for sleeping
  The poisonous shade;

Some faint and drooping
  Have sunk on the road;
And the strong limbs are stooping,
  Borne down by their load.

Like the dreams of the morn,
  The song-birds are fled;
But the vultures are borne
  To the feast of the dead.

On! through wild land,
  Where no shelter is seen,
No friendly hand
  Whereon we may lean.

Landmarks are rare,
  And distant the goal;
And the gloom of despair
  Presses hard on the soul.

Evening droops o'er us,
  And low sinks the sun;
A desert before us;
  Return there is none.

Where shall the weary rest,
  Wandering lonely?
Peace in the earth's cold breast
  Dwells, and there only.

Loss is our gain,
  And sorrow our mirth;
Trouble and pain
  Are born of the earth.

Part II.

"But now they desire a better country."

All things are vain
  We pursue from our birth;
While we cease not to strain
  For the things of the earth,—

For the fruits that are fair,
  But to ashes will turn,
For the bowers, all bare
  When noontide shall burn,—

For the flowers that fade,—
  For the fountains that fail,—
For the wealth that when weighed
  Grows light in the scale.

How shall we 'scape from sin
  With its false treasure?
How shall we hope to win
  Lastinger pleasure?

Where shall we find a guide,—
 We the forsaken,—
Never to quit our side,
 Ne'er be mistaken?

Eastward our journey lies;
 There in our youth,
Ere on our souls arise
 Mists of untruth,

If we but fix our eyes,
 Clear though afar,
Through the red morning skies
 Shineth our star.

Few eagle-sighted
 Long hold it in view;
But the path it has lighted
 Is steadfast and true.

As the track which a beacon
 Flings far o'er the lake,
With no moonlight to weaken,
 No ripple to shake.

If the foot goes astray,—
  If turns backward the gaze,—
Though childhood's fair ray
  Be lost in the haze,—

Though desert and burning
  The way we must go,—
Though the steps of returning
  Be painful and slow,—

Even yet for our leading
  A token shall shine,
From the east still proceeding,—
  A Cross for a sign.

And, when, weary with striving,
  The stout heart is bent,—
When the scattered surviving
  Are feeble and spent,—

Though dying and tender
  The sunlight has set,
The East with its splendour
  Is glorious yet;

Till their eye waxes clearer,
  Whose pulses are cold,—
And nearer and nearer
  The city of gold.

There shall they reign
  O'er a purified earth:
Why wander in vain,
  O redeemed from your birth?

The Days of Old.

THE days of old, the days of old,
  The times for aye departed,—
When dames were fair, and knights were bold,
  And lovers constant-hearted;
When magic barks o'er summer seas
  Swept with the voice of song,
And fairy music on the breeze
  Was softly borne along.

The days of old, the days of old,
  With deeds of heroes rife,—
When truth was valued more than gold,
  And honour more than life:
They went not selfish on their way,
  No care or thought for others;
If on a breast the red cross lay,
  Be sure it was a brother's.

The days of old, the days of old,
  The days of faith and truth,—
When love was free, and help unsold,
  And earth was in her youth;
Before by deed and thought and speech
  The electric chain was riven,
That binds our spirits each to each,
  And all of us to heaven.

The days of old, the days of old,
  The days of noble deed,—
When champions rode by wood and wold
  To succour all at need.
They stayed not then to count the cost
  At which the help was wrought;
What though by tarrying there were lost
  The prize so dearly sought,—
What though the way were drear and long,
  No hope of gain or fame,—
That these were weak, their foes were strong,
  It was sufficient claim.

The days of old, the days of old,—
  Ere minstrels' fees were stinted;
When songs were sung, and tales were told,
  But speeches were not printed;

When Nature all was fresh and glad,
  Her richest gifts in store,—
And poets found not others had
  Their happiest thoughts before;
War Correspondents sent no views
  With "should" and "had" and "if" in,
Nor artists published in the News
  The last-encountered griffin.

The days of old, the days of old,—
  When mansions were not rented;
Nor cheer with niggard hand was doled,
  Nor marriage-deeds invented;
The mirth and laughter never flagged;
  The wine passed round in flagons;
And every knight of fame had bagged
  His brace or two of dragons;
While, if his wishes sought a crown
  As settlement in life,
They offered in the nearest town
  A princess for a wife.

The days of old, the days of old,—
  When freedom loved the heather;
When outlaws never caught a cold,—
  Whate'er the greenwood weather;

And, if the leech should recommend
  A change of air as needed,
In packing up they need not spend
  The fortnight which preceded;
No care had they to search about
  For lodgings light and airy,
But turned some old enchanter out,
  Or feasted with a fairy.
Obedient genii in a night
  A crystal hall erected,
Or just as soon transferred the site,
  If vested rights objected.

The days of old, the days of old,—
  When right was rule alone,
Before the Codes were manifold,
  Or cramming yet was known:
In their own cause they made defence,
  Nor paid a lawyer's fee,
Nor (save the pugilistic sense)
  Were e'er in Chancery;
Each champion in his sword conveyed
  A perfect legislation;
And Orientals were not made

A branch of education,—
Yet, if, in plain or mountain glen,
(No matter what his nation)
A Christian met a Saracen,
They held a conversation,—
Which clearly shows our modern lights
Are greatly overrated,
Since neither Pagans now nor knights
Are half so educated :—
But gone are now the ancient wise;
Learning doth all her aid refuse;
When shall an Œdipus arise
To read us the "Fonetik Nuz?"

A Dream.

C'est une vallée verte et belle,—
Where it lies I may not tell,
Sive sit in Tempe, vel
Far beyond the sea,
Là où l'île Hespérienne
Holds a rest for perfect men,
Hosōn erga kala en
Les jours de la vie.

Ita tamen fit, ut sæpe,
When my eyes are worn and sleepy,
Se upabaner samīpe
Pass I in my dream
Sur un char des vents je saute,
And through fleecy clouds I float
On thæt æthele gemōt
Mibb'ney hamm' lākīm.

Kai entautha hē selēnē
Clarè splendet ac serenè,
"Ala ghusni 'lyāsimīni,
Und des Sommers See:
And the placid waters brighten
Wo die Elfenschifflein gleiten,
Atque inter Nymphas Triton
Sings across the bay.

Dāloṅ meṅ se kabhī bīnā,
Con armonia divina,
Arboreta per amœna
Rend ses tristes sons;
Where the lamps of living flame,
Que la fée du bocage aime,
Yeman prānsampanna hem,
Pharpharāte hoṅ.

Soon, too soon, must break the spell!
Traum verschwindend allzu schnell!
Vision frêle autant que belle!
Oh that I might sleep on,
"Ala 'ddawām ki bibīnam,
Suprà, cœlum tam serenum,
Nīche, desham shokahīnam,
Hōs ekeinon kēpon!

In the preceding lines there are specimens of fourteen languages. Verses 1, 5, 8, 13, 28, 30, and 35, are French; 2, 4, 6, 10, 12, 14, 21, 24, 29, 33, and 36, are English; 3, 9, 18, 23, 27, and 38, are Latin; 7, 17, and 40, are Greek; 11 and 31 are Bengali; 15 is Anglo-Saxon; 16 is Hebrew; 19 is Arabic; 20, 22, and 34, are German; 25 is Hindi; 26 is Italian; 32 is Urdu; 37 is Persian; and 39 is Sanscrit.

In reading the Oriental languages, the vowels are pronounced as in Italian, except that ă is like ŭ in English (but in Bengali like ŏ); the consonants are pronounced much as in English (but in Bengali y is like j, and s like sh; ṅ is nasal.

The following is a literal translation of the lines:—

It is a green and beautiful valley,—
Where it lies I may not tell,
Whether it be in Tempe, or
Far beyond the sea,
Where the Western Island
Holds a rest for perfect men,
Whose deeds were honourable in
The days of their life.
Thus however it happens, that often,
When my eyes are worn and sleepy,
Near to that garden
Pass I in my dream;
On a chariot of the winds I leap,
And through fleecy clouds I float
To the noble assembly
Of the sons of the kings.

And there the moon
Shines brightly and serenely,
On the branch of the jasmine
    And the summer sea:
And the placid waters brighten
Where the little fairy-boats glide,
And among the nymphs Triton
    Sings across the bay.
From among the branches sometimes the lute,
With divine harmony,
Through the pleasant groves
    Gives forth its sad sounds;
Where the lamps of living flame,
Which the woodland fairy loves,
Like gold possessed of life,
    May be twinkling.
Soon, too soon, must break the spell!
Dream vanishing all too quickly!
Vision frail as beautiful!
    Oh, that I might sleep on,
So that I may constantly see,
Above, a heaven thus calm,
Beneath, a country free from sorrow,
    As that garden!

ALBUM VERSES.

"Weep sore for Him that goeth away."

[A lady, whose sister was about to start for India, took up the Bible to try the "Sortes," and opened on Jeremiah xxii. 10.]

Weep for her that goeth,
  Ye who tarry here;
Every breeze that bloweth
  Bringeth doubt and fear:
Dangers may be nearest
  When they seem to sleep;
None to guard our dearest;—
  Therefore do we weep.

Mornings springing brightly
  Bring a cheerless day;
Sudden frosts may nightly
  Chill the flowers away;

Life is frail and fleeting;
  Fate is dark and deep;
Parting brings no meeting;—
  Mortals, we must weep.

Earth's a desert only,
  Where apart we roam;
If we journey lonely,
  We shall meet at home.
They who sow in sorrow
  Shall in gladness reap;
Bright shall break the morrow;—
  Christians, cease to weep.

On the Christening of an Infant in India.

NOVEMBER 15, 1857.

Born in a season of sorrow and strife,
With trouble and tumult and terror rife,
How shall we read, dear child, thy life?

How shall we shape our words to pray
That the seven best gifts [266] of wisdom may
Descend as the dews on thy brow this day?

Bold shalt thou be, as they who fell,
Striving so nobly and so well
To the aid of the leaguered citadel.

Tender withal, as the spirits brave
Who sought not their lives *alone* to save,—
Who stayed by the weaker—to share their grave.

Hopeful be thou, as those who stood
'Midst thousands thirsting for their blood,
Cheerful through evil and through good.

Faithful, as they who chose to die,—
Who put the proffered safety by,—
Who dared not live and their Lord deny.

Prudent, as those in whose wise command
The scattered spots of safety stand,
Like beacon-towers in a flooded land.

Just shall thou be to redeem the right,
As the vengeful arm of England's might,
Crushing the felon ranks in fight.

Temperate be thou ever, as they
Who slacked not their hand the guilty to slay,
But torture with torture would not repay.

Grace, a sevenfold grace be thine;
Gifts of the earth and gifts divine,
All good things in thy lot combine!

Be thou in soul as in race thou art,—
Be thou thy parents' counterpart,
With thy father's head and thy mother s heart!

On the Death of the Same.

(DECEMBER 9, 1857.)

I saw beside its parent stem
  A sapling springing fair;
I passed; again I sought for them;
  The sapling was not there.

Oh! sadly did the parent tree
  Her golden tresses shed;
So sharp a pang of agony
  Their roots had severèd.

Yet afterward I saw her smile
  More sweetly than before,
And towards the heaven as other-while
  She spread her golden store.

For dreams the plant we held so dear
  In brighter gardens show;
And graces nipped so early here
  In perfect beauty blow.

But with the soil where once it grew
  It sympathizes yet;
The stem from which its life it drew
  It never can forget.

Through secret rills its fostering care
  Shall heavenly dew convey,
And breathing down the fragrant air
  Shall life and love repay.

To Henrietta.

Let me write a line, and send it to my pet, a certain friend of mine, whose name is
But can I succeed? It would task a veteran in verse, indeed, to rhyme of
Still I think I'll try; whatever etiquette, a strong desire have I to write to
O Darjeeling dear, to you I owe a debt, a heavy debt,—for here I met with
When I think of hill, rock and rivulet, arise within me still thoughts of
Eyes so deep and blue; hair of glossy jet; a prettier picture who could find than
As to birds the gun, as to fish the net, a danger to each one would be
At your sunny smile the grumbler most inveterate would cease awhile to mope, my
Gladly would the sage leave his books and metaphysics, I engage, for sake of

I would undertake, through the cold and wet, a journey, for
the sake of seeing
Happy should I prove, could I only get a lady for my love
like to
May this many a day nothing vex or fret a spirit light and
gay as is
Never may there live one who would abet a word or look to
give pain to
Should I liken you to lark or violet? a flower of lovely hue,
or bird, my
Birds in gloomy skies tune their flageolet: a mind content
and wise may yours be,
Flowers blossom gay though by thorns beset: a creature
pure as they be you, O
Till your friends declare that they never met a girl so sweet
and fair, and good as
Gazing on the snow, as her birthday set, a wish I felt to
know the fate of
Hoping to discern happier, and yet a happier, return for
my
Pure as snow, her heart, like an amulet, avert all evil part
from my
But, as blushed the snow in the rays, so let affection's rosy
glow spring for

Far beneath her lie mists of vain regret! above, in cloudless sky, move my
—But these rhymes if I prolong until etcetera,—at last good-by must come to
Yes, I must depart! Do not you forget a warm and faithful heart, darling

HENRIETTA!

On receiving a Glow-worm from a Lady.

A GIFT, a gift of thine!
  Not on the coral stem,
Not in the diamond mine,
  It grew,—this living gem.
Ever some sheltered lair,
  'Mid ferns and mosses green,
Apart from gaud and glare,
  Concealed its modest sheen.
Dost thou true friendship need?
  Oh, leave the world's false light:
No gem so fair, so dead,
  Ever as cold as bright.
Life glows in friendships nursed in gentler ways;
Let me find such a friend, whose name this rhyme displays.

On the Death of Amy.

I AM sent to thee on my swiftest wing,
Belovèd as thou art;
A golden crown I bring,
From the Treasures of the King,
Though thou see but my deadly dart.

There be other crowns of as precious ore,
Which the conquering warriors win:
But sad the wounds and sore,
Which they who wear them bore,
As they strove with the hosts of Sin.

There be other faces as innocent
In the presence of the King;
But to lead thee I am sent,
Where thy Lord before thee went,
Perfect through suffering.

Belovèd, indeed, by the gift I bear:
    Is not my gift the best?
So I kiss thy forehead fair,
And I smooth thy golden hair,
    And I hush thee into rest.

Sonnet on the Same.

If that betrothal, half in lightness said,
Had been remembered in the after-tide,
Thou might'st perchance have claimed in me a guide.
Had earthly harm assailed thy gentle head;
But now the guidance may be thine instead,
And thine that whispered warning at my side:
For thou hast learnt a world of wisdom wide,
Which in no land of living men is read;
And thou canst calmly look on darker ways
Than mortal innocence unhurt could bear.
Thy loving eyes with strength anointed were,
What time, pure heart, they saw those glory-rays
Whereon thine angel's face doth ever gaze:
Beloved, guide me yet to win thy welcome there.

To a Godchild.

(EASTER MONDAY, APRIL 1.)

EVER round thy peaceful bed
  Troops of angel-guards attend:
Heaven upon thy favoured head
  Endless store of blessings send.
Let thy month, the month of Love,
  Crown for thee her opening day:
Let thy saddest sorrows prove
  April showers, to pass away.
Rainbow of a smiling heaven,
  Easter-gift, we clasp thee fast,
Welcome more that thou art given
  After tears of trouble past.
Thus would I, distraught and blind,
  Send thee blessings o'er the sea?
Oh, but blessings may'st thou find
  Not as seemeth best to me!

Sonnet,

TO A LADY ON HER LAST BIRTHDAY IN INDIA.

THEY say that India's sun shall shine no more
Upon the opening promise of thy year;
That gentler hours have gifts for thee in store,
Among the mellowing woods of Kent, or near
Fields waving pleasantly with golden ear
And scented hops, our England's vintage, or
Where Thames by cedared lawns flows soft and clear,
Or where sweet Devon crowns her flowery shore.
What need to speak of exile past and done?
So may thy children's voices greet thy name
Through many an autumn holiday; but we,
Whose friends pass homeward from us one by one,—
What joy for us this side the severing sea,
Save that on all the stars look down the same?

Charade.

ON THE MARRIAGE OF SOPHIA CATHERINE SLADEN.

In *my second*, hid from day,
Dark and dread the monster lay;
Far across the wasted plain
Withered trees and blasted grain
Felt the reptile's poisoned breath.—
What from Sin can spring but Death?

Sadder yet the slaughter-trace
Nearer round that evil place,
Maiden garb besmirched and rent,
Raven tresses gore-besprent.—
What has earth so young and fair
The destroyer turns to spare?

Therefore do the mourning cries
From the white-walled city rise:

From the king upon his throne
Each hath lost his loved, his own.—
Ancient conqueror is the Grave:
Not e'en Love is strong to save.

Now in virgin-white arrayed,
As beseems a royal maid,
Forth along that path of woe
Lonely must the princess go:
Yet she will not stay nor fly.—
Well, for those she loves, to die.

Blanched her cheek, and downcast eye
Lest she earlier should espy
What she knoweth, soon or late,
Must her onward steps await.—
Sharper pain, the sweeter rest;
That which is decreed is best.

Lo! across the sultry haze
Whence the sudden armour blaze?
Who the champion rides this way,
Glorious in his war array?—

When all hope is turned to dust,
Cometh help to them that trust.

How shall mortal warrior hope
With unearthly foe to cope?
Scales of brass and throat of flame,
Strength that armies could not tame.—
Vain on earthly arms to lean;
Best are those which are not seen.

Only let his heart be pure,
Words be true, and thrust be sure;
Then that fiery breath shall yield,
Quenched before his red-cross shield.
So against the fiend accurst
He prevaileth to *my first*.

Thou whose life this day hath crowned,
In whose name *my whole* is found,—
Prove thyself like Una's knight,
Warrior ever brave and bright;
So may'st thou an Una find
Her whose lot with thine is twined!

Find her as her name is writ,
Wise of soul with heavenly wit;
Find her as the letters paint,
Pure in heart as virgin saint:
So let all your days be blest,—
Latest, still the happiest!

To a Friend.

ON HER COMING OF AGE (WRITTEN AT BOMBAY).

Each night the western winds arise,
  Vexed, shrill, complaining, from the sea:
Each night the stars, calm as thine eyes,
  Look on my lonely tent and me.
Yet, as their orbs roll slowly by,
  Night hushes down that restless wail;
Then, from his rocky distance, I
  Hear Ocean's solemn, ceaseless tale.
Oh, thus may perfect womanhood
  Make all thy days secure and still!
Peace crown thy life with amplest good!
  Spring's promise Summer's fruits fulfil!
On earth long joys be thine! Yet, through them all,
Nearer and clearer still the eternal voices fall!

On the Death of a Friend.

In a vision once again
 Saw I her in beauty's bloom,
Ere they made her denizen
 Of the sad and silent tomb;
Ere, as falls on Nature's face,
When the sun hath run his race,
When the darkness comes apace,
Fell upon our souls that sudden gloom.

Still as beautiful and bright,
 Gentle eye and softest tress,
Hallowing meaner things with light
 Of her passing loveliness.
Often in that queenly face
Hath my fancy loved to trace
Shadowed forth each inward grace,
All around her path that wont to bless.

Losing her, the joys we knew
  All the joy which crowned them lack:
And our hopes of brightest hue,
  Losing her, are hung with black.
Yet, if words of mine had power
To renew the vanished hour,
To restore the withered flower,—
Yet I would not speak to call her back.

For she sleepeth calm and still,
  By the ancient river's tide,
Where the sun may shine at will
  'Mid the branches waving wide.
Wherefore speak of her as clay,
Whom the angels bore away,
Breathing now a purer day
Than hath bard in loftiest vision eyed?

Hath she not a message now
  To the friends she loved on earth,
Sent to soothe the throbbing brow,
  Sent to calm the careless mirth,
When in thankless paths they rove
Sent to draw our hearts above?
Oh! beside her angel love
All the mortal did shall pale in worth.

Sonnet.

As one who, journeying through a burning zone,
  Unwitting chances on a fountain fair,
  Girt all around with trees of fruitage rare,
Upon whose branches birds of sweetest tone
Salute the echoes of that valley lone,—
  Tears to his eyelids start, and thoughts of prayer
  And thankfulness rise heavenward, unaware:
Cast among strangers so was I, unknown,—
With warmest welcome met, with friendly eyes;
  And I thenceforth have ever found a friend
    To feel my griefs, and in my joys rejoice.
Should time decay my brighter memories,
  O'er all things else his empire may extend,—
    Not thy sweet eyes, and not thy gentle voice.

To Bertha Margaret.

BRIGHT are the dewdrops, the jewels of morning,
  Each a gem for the flowers' queen ;
Rainbows in fragments the blossoms adorning.
  They rejoice in the sun's new sheen.
Health and loveliness from them welling,
  As the dewdrops may'st thou too be,
Making a paradise round thy dwelling,
  All thine hours of mirth and glee !

Raindrops all in the sun may not glitter ;
  Garden and woodland some nourish not ;
Under the sea-waves, lonely and bitter,
  Exile and darkness their dreary lot.[267]
Raindrop-like, be content with thy station :
  Ill and good come alike from above :
Trust through the waters of life's tribulation ;
  Even the billows are guided by Love.

Bright are the pearldrops, the treasures of Ocean,
  Each a gem for a crownèd king:
Numbered for monarchs with care and devotion;
  Theirs in the day of reckoning.
Happiness lasteth not here till the morrow:
  All earth's brightest is but for a day;
Low must they pass through the waters of sorrow,
  Light who inherit that fades not away.

Charade.

BRIGHTLY glowed the morning sun,
  As the Monks of Bangor sang;[268]
But, before *my first* was done,
  Battle closed and arrows rang.

Red *my next* was stained with gore,
  Ere the noon had reached its height.
When the heathen's onset bore
  Britain's chiefs to hurrying flight.

O'er the traces of *my whole*
  Night a veil of pity cast;
But, till suns shall backward roll,
  Rule from Arthur's race had passed.

To Edith Mary.

HAPPINESS and bitterness,
  Who hath these united?
Parting with the first caress
  Of the newly plighted,
Silver with the raven tress,
Roses in their summer dress
  With the autumn-blighted?

Bitterness and happiness,
  Well they are not parted:
Balm the wounded souls to bless
  Which for guilt have smarted,
Peace for those who sins confess,
Hope and comfort in distress
  For the lonely-hearted.

Must they mingle thus for aye
  Failure with endeavour?
Life and beauty from decay
  One alone can sever,—
Where no night shall close the day,
Where the tears are wiped away
  From our eyes for ever.

Crambo.

[Question—Where were you brought up ? Word to be introduced—Pundit.]

WHERE o'er the storied shrines of saints
Religion weds with Beauty;
Where to young hearts Tradition paints
The loyal path of duty;
Where Statesmen and where Prelates found
The earliest steps of learning;
Where, met again in hallowed ground,
Their frames to dust are turning:
Where, if aught base or vile abode,
The very air had shunned it;
Where founts of learning ever flowed,
Enough to make a Pundit.

Bridal Verses.

ROSES wove her bridal wreath,
 Roses red of June ;
All the flowers of May
Lingered but to say,
 Maiden, thou must leave us soon !

All the daughters of the sea
 Round her path would smile,
As their amethyst eyes
Laughed to sunny skies,
 And they sang sweet songs the while.

Spring and summer joined their hands
 O'er her gentle head ;
Earth and heaven vied
Thus to bless the bride,
 From her English birthplace sped.

Sunny days on Devon's shore,
  Bring a sunny life!
Love and joy increase!
Happiness and peace
  Keep the footsteps of the wife!

A Prayer.

Lord, let all Thy love can bring
  On her flow with bounteous grace;
Under Thy protecting wing
  Is her sure abiding place.
Safely may her footsteps go,
  As a child would fearless tread,
Watched by loving friends below,
  And Thine angels overhead.

Though there be who love her well,
  Earthly arms are weak and frail;—
Raging waves may storm and swell;
  Faith is fixed, and cannot fail.
In Thy favour from above
  Endless blessings keep mine own,—
Life a path of faith and love,—
  Death a gate to joys unknown!

Allahabad.

NOVEMBER, 1865.

AROUND thy birth-place glide
  The sisters blue and brown;
Each rolls her laughing tide,
  The weary land to crown:
But they may not abide;
  Their waters ebb away;
And thou, too, from our side
  Didst pass as they.

The trees, that saw thy birth,
  Were bright with fragrant bloom:
Their blossoms strewed the earth,
  And knew not of thy tomb:
The season of their mirth
  Was brief, however gay;
And thou, too, from our hearth
  Didst fade as they.

The streams which winter dries
  Shall swell with melting snows,
And summers new shall rise
  As other summers rose :
But thou didst reach the skies,
  Nor know a wintry day ;
And thou shalt glad our eyes
  Once more as they.

Mussoorie.

SEPTEMBER, 1867.

COVER the eyes that shone so bright :
Hold the violet, fingers slight,
And the windflower and everlasting white.

Raise him up in the misty eve :
Let those eyes that awhile must grieve
Endless sunshine through tears perceive.

Strength of the everlasting hill,
Land of the rock, and mist, and rill,
Open the casket our jewel must fill.

Under the oak tree lay him to sleep :
Is there not comfort for those that weep ?
Sadness to sow, but joy to reap ?

Sonnet.

Kind breezes waft them on their homeward way
Across the perilous sea and sultry strait;
Thou ship, sail swiftly with thy priceless freight;
Hide, gentle clouds, the force of flaming day;
Angels, on innocence and love that wait,
Relax no care for sin of mine, that they,
In safety brought to happy meeting, may
New mercies with new thankfulness relate.
Easter is come, but where my sweetest rose?
Easter is come, but where my opening flower?
My Lent is lengthened through the joyous days:
I watch, but still the brimming river flows.
Light of my life, may the endless Easter hour
Yet find us hand in hand to sing our songs of praise.

NOTES.

NOTES.

[1] The sun.

[2] Ghī: clarified butter. Gur: molasses.

[3] Gates of Gangā: Haridwār (Anglicè, Hurdwar) where the Ganges enters the plain country.

[4] Umā: a name of Durgā, Gauri or Pārvatī, wife of Shiva, and, in one of her births, daughter of Daksha. Her attendant is the lion.

[5] Kailāsa: the paradise of Shiva,—the "Calasay" of Southey.

[6] Rudras: demigods, attendant on Shiva.

[7] Muni: a sage.—Nārada, though a holy personage, often appears in a discreditable situation, and is cursed with a restless spirit, which leads him to wander about, mischief-making by his news. He is the instructor of the Gandharbas, or heavenly musicians,—the "Glendoveers" of Southey.

[8] Shiva bears on his forehead a crescent and the river Ganges. He wears a necklace of skulls, and girdle, bracelets, &c. of serpents. He is often naked in other respects, except that he smears his body with ashes, and flings over his shoulders a raw elephant's hide. He is attended by bloodthirsty goblins, and is the patron of magical rites in burning grounds, of crazy fanatics, &c.

[9] The Deer's Head is the constellation Orion.

[10] The Koïl is the Indian cuckoo.

[11] The Dhāk, silk cotton, and coral trees are covered with red blossoms before the leaves appear.

[12] Ananga, the bodiless,—a common name of Kāma, explained by this legend. (*See* also "Destruction of the Yādavas:" stanza 40.)

[13] Tāraka; a demon who was not to be overcome, except by a son of Shiva, who had then neither son nor wife.

[14] Himavān, the snowy; the same as Himālaya, the house of snow.

[15] Meru; the mountain on which stand the palaces of the gods.

[16] Five arrows, barbed with five different flowers.

[17] Rudrāksha, Eleocarpus ganitrus. Shiva's head is adorned with the moon and the Ganges.

[18] The fish is the banner of Kāma.

[19] Pārvatī, the daughter of the mountain (Himālaya), in which character the Queen of Shiva was born again after her death in the sacrificial fire. (*See* the "Sacrifice of Daksha.")

[20] There is a red lotus as well as the white.

[21] Kārtikeya, the god of war.

[22] The centre eye in the forehead, always a mark of Shiva.

[23] Heart-born, another of Kāma's names.

[24] Suras—gods or demigods, of whom Indra is the king.

[25] Asuras (those who are not Suras),—their opponents, the Titans, or demons.

[26] Shesha: *see* stanzas 44 and 45 of the "Destruction of the Yādavas."

[27] The tortoise is the second Avatāra of Vishnu.

[28] The chariot of the sun is drawn by a horse with seven heads; according to other accounts, by seven horses. (*See* "Fourth Avatāra," stanza 39.)

[29] Airāvata, Indra's elephant.

[30] Kāmadhenu or Surabhi: *see* "Destruction of the Yādavas," stanza 4.

[31] Pārijāta, one of the five trees of Swarga or Paradise. (*See* "Hymn to Indra.")

[32] Disc, Sudarshana: *see* "Destruction of the Yādavas," stanza 5.

[33] Shiva's bow: *see* Introduction to "The last ordeal of Sītā."

[34] The Apsarasas. The resemblance to the legend of Venus Aphrodite is striking.

[35] Dhanwantari, physician of the gods.

[36] Lakshmī: *see* "Fourth Avatāra," stanzas 7 and 8.

[37] Shiva is called Nilakantha or Blue-Throat. (*See* "Ambā," stanza 6.)

[38] Amrita. The same word as Ambrosia, the draught of immortality.

[39] The reckoning of the fourteen jewels is not always the same. Some lists omit the Sun and Vishnu's quoit, counting the nymphs and the poison among the jewels. Instead of the horse of the Sun and the bow of Shiva, they mention those of Indra. Now the first incarnation was the fish which guided the ark over the waters of the deluge; and this of the tortoise, which was the second, is said by some to have been manifested in order to recover the treasures lost in the ocean during the flood. To this tradition the bow of Indra, which is the rainbow, seems appropriate. The fatal discovery of wine immediately succeeding the deluge is also a remarkable point in the legend.

[40] Rāhu, the head, and Ketu, the tail of the dragon, are the ascending and descending nodes in astronomical mythology. And hence the origin of eclipses.

[41] The followers of Vishnu of course exalt him to the chief place in the Triad.

[42] One tradition of Hindū cosmogony represents the whole universe to be enclosed in a golden shell; hence it is commonly called the egg of Brahmā.

[43] During the interval between two cycles of creation, Vishnu is said to sleep on the chaotic ocean, resting on Shesha, the thousand-headed king of the serpents.

[44] Here Brahmā and Shiva are represented as merely other manifestations of Vishnu.

[45] The fifth Avatāra, or incarnation, is that of the dwarf, who begged from Bali a boon of three paces of land. In the first, he took the earth, and, in the second, heaven; but, on Bali's submission, he refrained from depriving him of Pātāla, the subterraneous region, where Bali accordingly reigns still.

The third Avatāra was that of the boar, who dived and brought up on his tusks the earth and the Vedas, both sunk in the ocean by the giant Hiranyāksha (the Ermaccasen of Southey.)

The first Avatāra was the fish, which preserved Manu at the time of the deluge. The vessel of the king was fastened to his horn, and guided safely through the ocean.

[46] Parashu Rāma (or Rāma with the axe), Rāmachandra, and Balarāma, were the sixth, seventh, and eighth (or ninth) Avatāras. The last was armed with a ploughshare; he is brother of Krishna, and husband of Revatī. The first destroyed the Kshatriyas, or military caste, twenty-one times, in revenge for the murder of his father, Jamadagni the hermit; and with his axe he opened a way for the Ganges, through the Himālaya, or house of snow. Rāmachandra, of the solar dynasty, was Prince of Ayodhyā (Oudh), the modern Fyzābād. His wife Sitā was carried off by the ten-headed giant Rāvana, who reigned in Lankā (Ceylon); Rāma pursued him with an army of bears and monkeys (probably the wild tribes of the south, as the Aryan race and Brāhman religion were long confined to the north of the Vindhya Mountains); to rescue Sitā, they are supposed to have built Adam's Bridge from the continent to the island.

[47] Sitā is an incarnation of Lakshmī, who reigns with Vishnu as his queen, upon the milky ocean.

[48] Lakshmī, goddess of prosperity, was one of the fourteen treasures obtained from the sea when the gods and demons churned it to obtain the Amrita, or water of immortality (the demons, however, for their share were put off with wine); the churning staff was Mount Mandara resting on the tortoise, the second Avatāra; and the rope was the serpent Shesha held at the head by the demons and at the tail by the gods. So great was Lakshmī's beauty that the guardians of the eight points of the compass became her suitors; but she selected Vishnu. (*See* "The Churning of the Ocean.")

When Sitā was rescued from Rāvana, she underwent the ordeal of fire to prove her purity, to which also all the gods bore witness, raining flowers upon her. (*See* " The Last Ordeal of Sītā.")

[49] The Vimāna is the animated vehicle of the gods. (Southey's "ship of the gods.")

[50] Krishna is by some considered the ninth Avatāra; by others, who look on Buddha as the eighth, assumed to mislead the wicked, he is regarded as an emanation from the Deity, distinct from, and superior to the ten Avatāras. He was fostered among the herdsmen of Vrindā, to conceal him from the usurper Kansa, who knew that Krishna was destined to destroy him. One of the names of Vishnu is " yellow-robed."

[51] Krishna means dark-blue; and he is always represented of a black colour, as is well known from the representations of Jagannāth.

[52] Golden-mailed—Hiranyakashipu, or golden armour—the " Errenen " of Southey.

[53] Diti was mother of the Daityas, or Titans.

[54] Gurus are spiritual teachers.

[55] It has been suggested that the tortoise which supports the world—the third Avatāra—may be a tradition of the great fossil tortoise found in India. Can this be an allusion to the coal epoch ?

[56] Himavān, the snowy, is the same as Himālaya, the house of snow.

[57] Saints—the Prachetasas—ten patriarchs who spent 10,000 years in the sea in meditation, during which time the trees overspread the earth. On their return they destroyed the forests by the wind and flame of their anger.

[58] Hiranyakashipu : *see* stanza 12.

[59] Hari is the most common of the names of Vishnu.

[60] Mahādeva, the great god,—Shiva.

[61] Varuna is god of the sea.

[62] Vaikuntha is Vishnu's paradise.

[63] Soma is the god of the moon. During the former half of the month,

the moon is supposed to be filled with amrita or nectar, which is drunk by the gods and fathers during the latter half.

64 The sun's chariot is drawn by seven green horses, the seven days of the week.

65 Stanza 45. The tenth Avatāra, yet to come, is that of Kalkī, or the swordsman mounted on the white horse.

66 Nārada : *see* note 7, on the "Sacrifice of Daksha."

67 Vakul : mimusops elengi.

68 It seems to have been a favourite amusement of the Hindū ladies to unite by a marriage ceremony two of the trees in their gardens.

69 Ashoka : the Jonesia Asoca, said to flower when touched by a lady's foot. (*See* note 134 to the "Destruction of the Yādavas," stanza 11.)

70 Chakravāka, the Brāhminī duck ; the Indian emblem of conjugal affection.

71 Koīl, the Indian cuckoo.

72 Parashu Rāma : *see* note 46 to the "Fourth Avatāra," stanza 6.

73 A wife may not wear her ornaments in her husband's absence. Clasping the bracelet is a part of the marriage ceremony.

74 "Chosen by the crown of Raghu's race :" literally, the tilaka, or mark impressed on the forehead at consecration. The powder with which it is made is still sent to the Hindū princes, on their accession, by the Rānā of Udipur, who claims descent from Rāma, and is admitted to be the best blood in India. Raghu was great-grandfather of Rāma.

75 Ashoka : Jonesia Asoca.

76 Tall tree : the famous fig-tree at Allahabad, where the Jumna and Ganges mingle their waters, blue and brown.

77 Shukra or Ushanas, regent of the planet Venus, and spiritual guide of the Titans ; as Vrihaspati, or Jupiter, is of the gods.

78 King Vrishaparvan, King of the Dānavas, and father of Sharmishthā.

[79] Suras, the demi-gods and constant foes of the Titans. It is curious how often in Indian legends, as in the story of Promethens, our sympathies are excited rather by the Titans than by their successful rivals. They are always worsted in the end of their conflicts, but seldom in fair fight. Sometimes a direct emanation from the superior gods takes place to save the Suras; sometimes they obtain the aid of warriors of human race; sometimes the Titans are defeated through a trick—through their unswerving fixity of purpose, or through being led into heresy and error by a god taking the shape of their teachers.

[80] The arrows of Kāma are barbed with five flowers. (*See* the "Song of the Koïl.")

[81] Every hour of the day had its allotted occupation for the Indian kings, and from the dramas it seems that the changes were announced in verse by the warders of the palace.

[82] It will of course be remembered that the Indian princes were not limited to a single queen.

[83] The name of Yadu is still preserved in the powerful tribe of the Jāts.

[84] Porus, the opponent of Alexander, is supposed to have been a namesake, if not a descendant of Puru.

[85] Kāshi is Benares.

[86] Bholānāth (the lord or husband of Bholā, one of the names of Pārvatī), and Mahādev (the great god), are titles of Shiva.

[87] In justice to the lady, it must be stated that the author of the *Prem Sāgar* misrepresented her story; indeed, there is scarcely a heroine of Indian mythology who is not represented as a model of wifely virtue. She was taken captive by King Bhīshma, who, however, dismissed her honourably when he found that she was a married woman. But her husband refused to receive one who had even been in the power of another; and it was for thus destroying her domestic happiness, that she sought for revenge upon Bhīshma.

[88] Vīnā is the Hindū lute.

[89] Indra is the god of the thousand eyes, and lord of paradise.

90 The chakor, bartavelle, or Greek partridge, is supposed to feed on the moonbeams.

91 Shiva, whose abode is on Mount Kailāsa, in the Himālayas, is usually represented riding on a white bull, with the crescent on his forehead, and the other emblems in the text.

92 The dark-blue colour of his throat was caused by his swallowing the poison, which threatened to consume the world, at the churning of the ocean. (*See* the ballad of that name.)

93 Swarga is Paradise; Indra its king.

94 Kuvera is the god of wealth, and possessor of the nine famous jewels.

95 Lakshmī is the goddess of fortune, and wife of Vishnu.

96 Ugrasena was King of the Yādavas, Krishna's tribe.

97 The Shrāddha is the funeral ceremonies.

98 Lankā and Rāvana: *see* note 46, on stanza 6 of "The Fourth Avatāra."

99 Rāma is Balarāma, brother of Krishna,—not Rāmachundra, the patron of Jāmbavat.

100 Hastināpur is on the Ganges, not far from Delhi.

101 Kauravas: *see* note 160, to stanza 34 of the "Destruction of the Yādavas."

102 Mithilā is Tirhut.

103 A kos is two miles.

104 The disc or quoit is Krishna's weapon.

105 Vasudeva was father of Krishna.

106 The Ocean-city is Dwārakā, on the coast of Kattiāwār, in Gujrāt, fabled to have been built on the ocean. (*See* "Destruction of the Yādavas," stanza 5.)

107 Bharata was the first sovereign who enjoyed universal empire, whence India is known as Bharatavarsha, the region of Bharata.

108 Manu was the Hindū Noah.

109 Yadu was the ancestor of the tribe to which Krishna belonged.

110 The Bartavelle, or Greek partridge, is supposed to feed on the moonbeams. The Indian simile, "The moon sees many night-flowers—the night-flower sees but one moon," is well known, having been published by Sir Wm. Jones, and imitated by Moore.

111 Fourteen jewels were gained from the ocean, when churned by the gods and demons. Mount Mandara was the churning stick, and the serpent Vāsuki was the rope; but the latter, wearied with the labour too long continued, emitted a poison which nearly consumed the world. There are other versions of the legend. (*See* the "Churning of the Ocean.")

112 The city is Dwārakā, situated on the coast of the peninsula of Gujrāt.

113 The Kalpa is one of the five trees of Swarga. (*See* "Hymn to Indra.")

114 Surabhi is the cow of plenty.

115 Vishnakarman was the architect of the gods.

116 The Yādavas were transported from Mathurā, when besieged by Jarāsantha.

117 Sudarshana is the animated discus of Vishnu.

118 The seven regions: *see* note to the "Moral of History."

119 Ugrasena was the king of the Yādavas.

120 The five trees, branches of which are placed in waterpots on festivals, are the Indian, the holy, and the wave-leaved fig-trees, the mango, and a kind of acacia.

121 Krishna was born to slay the tyrant Kaṇsa, who usurped the throne of his (Kaṇsa's) father, Ugrasena.

122 Krishna was an incarnation of Vishnu, who is usually represented seated on a lotus.

123 It had been foretold to Kaṇsa that he should be slain by the eighth son of Vasudeva and Devakī. Great precautions were therefore taken to slay the infant at the moment of birth; but, in spite of all, Vasudeva was enabled to convey the child to Nanda, chief of the herdsmen of Vraja, who brought him up.

[124] Yamunā is by the English written and pronounced Jumna.

[125] Yadu was the eldest son of Yayāti, but, with his brethren, was disinherited, and the crown conferred on the youngest, Puru, who had taken on him his father's decay, in exchange for his own youth. (*See* "Sharmishthā.")

[126] Rukminī (*see* note on "Rukminī"), Jāmbavatī (*see* "The Syamantak Jewel"), and Kālindī, were three of Krishna's eight queens.

[127] The waters of the Yamunā are blue and clear.

[128] Some of these similes are not very consonant with European ideas, as the comparison of the tapering back-hair to a snake, and the slow, languid step to an elephant's motion; but the latter especially is too universal a point of description, and too characteristic of Indian notions of elegance, to be omitted.

[129] The koïl is the Indian cuckoo, named from its note.

[130] The vimba is a small red gourd: the Momordica monadelpha.

[131] The champaka is a deliciously fragrant flower of the magnolia family, Michelia Champac.

[132] The rose is Persian, and would not be found in classical poetry, but it occurs in the corresponding passage of the Premsāgar.

[133] The colour of a smile is white in Indian poetry.

[134] The Ashoka (Jonesia Asoca) flowers when touched by a lady's foot. It has a beautiful scarlet blossom; but the leaves are at the end of the branches.

[135] The deer are always said to be captivated by music.

[136] Kālindī is the daughter of the Sun.

[137] Meru, where stand the palaces of the gods, is the North Pole.

[138] The king is often described under the emblem of a bull.

[139] The Yamunā, or Jumna, is also daughter of the Sun; indeed Kālindī is probably the river personified.

[140] The wife wears no ornaments while her husband is absent.

141 Vaikuntha is the heaven of Vishnu, as Swarga is of Indra.

142 The impostor was Paundraka, who in Kāshī, or Benares, asserted himself to be an incarnation of Vishnu. This points apparently to a schism among the Vaishnavas, the weaker party in which was supported by the followers of Shiva.

143 The Kali, or iron, age, dates from the death of Krishna.

144 Murāri means the enemy of Mura, who was a demon slain by Krishna.

145 Krityā was a female fiend, produced from the sacrificial fire by the incantations of the son of the King of Kāshī, to revenge the death of his father, who fell with his friend, King Paundraka. (*See* stanza 19.)

146 Sālava and the brothers of King Shishupāla, Vakradanta, and Vidūratha, made various attacks upon Dwārakā, to revenge the death of Shishupāla.

147 Dwivida was minister of Sālava.

148 Madhu was a demon slain by Vishnu.

149 Arjuna was third of the five Pāndava princes.

150 Balarāma was elder brother of Krishna ; his weapons were a pestle and ploughshare.

151 Paundrak : *see* stanza 19.

152 Rukmin, brother of Rukminī, led an army to rescue her, when Krishna carried her off. (*See* " Rukminī.")

153 Bāna : *see* stanza 38.

154 Anga is the country about Bhāgalpur.

155 The Apsarasas, or nymphs of Paradise, are wedded to warriors slain in battle. The expression does not mean choosers of those marked for slaughter, as in the Northern mythology, but choosers for themselves of the bravest warriors among those fallen in battle.

156 Prabhāsa is a place of pilgrimage near Somnāth, on the coast of Gujrāt.

157 The Meghadūta has, in a somewhat different reasoning,—

"The fairest portion of celestial birth,
Of Indra's paradise transferred to earth,
The last reward to acts of virtue given,
The only recompence then left to heaven."

158 Mace: *see* stanza 35.

159 Bhadrasena and Durgama were sons of Vasudeva. Chāru and Shruta were sons of Krishna. Prithu was a Yādava.

160 The hundred Kuru princes ruled in Hastināpura, (or the elephant city,) on the Ganges not far from Delhi. Duryodhana was the eldest of them, and his daughter was carried off by Sāmba, while making her public choice of a husband; the Kurus pursued and captured him.

161 A bend in the river Yamunā is said to have been caused by Balarāma, who drew her to him with his ploughshare, when she refused to change her course to bathe him.

162 Sāmba was dressed by his companions as a woman, and brought to the sages as a bride inquiring about her future offspring; the sages, incensed, replied, "A club, which shall destroy the race of Yadu."

163 Drona was father of Ashwatthāman, preceptor of the Kuru princes, and their helper in the war with the Pāndavas. (*See* stanza 47.)

164 Satyabhāmā, wife of Krishna, and daughter of Satrājit, had been wooed by Akrūra, Kritavarman, and Shatadhanwan, and the two former persuaded the latter to revenge his slight by the murder of Satrājit; Krishna revenged his death. (*See* the "Story of the Syamantak Jewel.")

165 Bāna, King of the Daityas or Titans, propitiated Shiva, and gained a thousand arms; but, finding no employment for them, he again requested an antagonist. Shiva gave him a flag, on the fall of which he would meet with an enemy, viz. Krishna, who came to rescue his grandson, Aniruddha, son of Pradyumna, from confinement, as Bāna had thrown him into chains on the discovery of his secret marriage with his daughter Ushā.

166 On the death of Satrājit (*see* stanza 36), Akrūra got possession of the jewel he had obtained from the Sun. (*See* the "Story of the Syamantak Jewel.")

[167] Pradyumna, son of Krishna and Rukminī, was an incarnation of Kāma, god of love, after he was reduced to ashes by Shiva. (*See* the "Song of the Koïl.")

[168] The royal families of India all belonged to the solar or lunar race. All were engaged in the great war between the Kurus and their cousins, the five Pāndava princes.

[169] Dāruka was Krishna's charioteer.

[170] Balarāma was an incarnation of Shesha, king of serpents.

[171] The Nāgas are the snake-gods who dwell in Pātāla, or the subterranean regions.

[172] Vishnu's paradise, Vaikuntha, is on the ocean of milk.

[173] Prithā was wife of Pāndu, and mother of the three eldest of the five princes.

[174] Vajra was son of Aniruddha.

[175] The tenth incarnation, yet to come, is Kalki, or the rider on the white horse.

[176] Durvāsas, the implacable sage, being offended by Krishna, foretold his death. A part of the club (*see* stanza 35) could not be ground to powder, and was thrown into the sea; but it was swallowed by a fish, and recovered by a hunter.

[177] The two great Indian epics are the Rāmāyana, said to have been written before Rāma's birth, and the Mahābhārata, or war of the Kaurava and Pāndava princes. (*See* stanza 43.)

[178] Rāvana, king of Lankā, or Ceylon, carried off Sītā, wife of Rāma. (*See* the "Last Ordeal of Sītā.")

[179] Yudhishthira, Bhīma, Arjuna, and the Twins, were the five princes. A sacrifice held by Yudhishthira, as paramount sovereign of India, caused much of the jealousy which led to the war.

[180] Siddhas are demigods who dwell in the middle air.

[181] The Ganges of heaven is the Milky Way.

182 The seven Saints, or Rishis, are the Great Bear.

183 Dhruva is the pole star.

184 Stanza 49 is taken from the description in Act v. of *Shakuntalā.*

185 Hemakūta, or Golden Peak, is the residence of Kashyapa and Aditi, the parents of the gods.

186 Kailāsa is the abode of Shiva—Southey's "silver mount of Calasay."

187 The sleep of the Universe is the chaos between two cycles of creation.

188 Indra, with his thunderbolt, leads the gods in their encounters with the demons.

189 The temple is said by some to be a portion of the original Dwārakā; its antiquity is certainly very great.

190 The children of the sage Bhrigu were persecuted by the sons of King Kritavīrya. From the wrath of Aurva, grandson of Bhrigu, proceeded a flame, which would have destroyed the world, had he not, on Brahmā's entreaty, confined it in the ocean; but the time comes when it shall burst its bonds.

191 Varuna is god of the sea.

192 The *five* elements of the Hindūs are each to be absorbed in the next grosser, and the last to be absorbed in the universal spirit.

193 Exemption from future birth is, according to Hindū philosophy, only to be obtained by the knowledge that this spirit pervades all things, and is, in fact, one with our own and with those of others,—and that consequently all things, good and evil, are equal.

194 Kālindī is the daughter of the Sun. (*See* "Destruction of the Yādavas," stanza 12.)

195 Sīmal, the silk cotton tree. Before its leaves come, it is a mass of large red blossoms, most brilliant in the sunshine.

196 Coral tree: Erythrina fulgens: Pārijāta.

197 Parrot bloom: Butea frondosa: Palāsha, from which the field of Plassey was named. Its orange scarlet pea flower is thought to resemble a parrot's beak, from which it derives its other name of Kinshuka.

[198] Koīl: the Indian cuckoo.

[199] Vaikuntha: Vishnu's paradise.

[200] Kalpa tree: the tree of heaven, which grants every wish.

[201] Padma bloom: the white lotus.

[202] The white water-lily, nymphæa esculenta, opens its blossoms by night, as the lotus does by day.

[203] Chakravāka (ki, fem.), the Brāhminī duck, the Indian emblem of conjugal affection. It is supposed to be under a curse, by which it is doomed to pass the night on the opposite bank of the river to its mate, to whom it calls the whole night through.

[204] The milky way.

[205] The Brāhmans, and also the two next classes, are solemnly invested with a thread, which, being considered a spiritual birth, gives them the title of twice-born. The simile, however, is scarcely Indian, as a Hindū would describe the Ganges as threefold, including its course in Pātāla.

[206] Sagara, purposing to perform an ashwamedha, or sacrifice of a horse, as an essential part of the ceremony set at liberty the horse, which was carried off by one of the serpents of Pātāla. The king directed his sons by his wife Sumati, 60,000 in number, to recover the steed. Their efforts, though unavailing, were enough to alarm the gods and demons, and to insure their destruction. After penetrating deep towards the subterranean regions, they came upon the horse grazing near Kapila, an incarnation of Vishnu as a sage, whom the sons of Sagara challenged as the thief. Kapila, incensed, reduced them all to ashes with a blast from his nostrils. Anshumat, the son of Asamanjas, the son of Sagara by his other wife, Keshinī, afterwards discovered the relics of his uncles, and learned from Garūra, their uncle, that the waters of the Ganges were necessary to procure them admission to heaven. Neither was Sagara, nor his successors, Anshumat and Dilīpa, able to effect the descent of Gangā, which was reserved for the son and successor of the latter, Bhagīratha. On the austerities of this prince successively propitiating Brahmā, Umā, and Mahādeva, the Ganges was by their power compelled to flow over the earth, following Bhagīratha to the sea, and thence to Pātāla, where the ashes of

his ancestors were laved by its waters. The Ganges was called Bhagirathī, in honour of the king, and the ocean termed Sāgara, as in Saugor Island, in commemoration of Sagara and his sons.

207 The Nāgas are snake-gods, who inhabit Pātāla, or the subterranean regions.

208 Maitreya is the pupil to whom the Vishnu Purāna is related by the sage, his instructor.

209 Manu is the Noah of the Hindūs.

210 There are in the Hindū cosmogony seven earths, each surrounded by its own ocean of a different composition.

211 Prithu was so famous for universal empire that the earth is from him commonly called Prithivī.

212 Sīmal is the silk cotton-tree. Its cotton is very white and beautiful, and shines like snow, after the crimson blossoms have fallen in early spring; but it is of no practical value.

213 Kārtavīrya, a patronymic of Arjuna, who conquered Rāvana, but was slain by Parashurāma.

214 Raghu was a famous prince of the solar dynasty, king of Ayodhyā, or Oudh, and ancestor of Rāma.

215 The inhabitants of Taurica Chersonesus, now the Crimea, offered on the altar of Diana all strangers shipwrecked on their coasts.

216 Iphigenia.

217 Endymion was a shepherd and astronomer, whence he is said to have been loved by Luna.

218 Hippolytus, son of Theseus, a hunter devoted to Diana, having unjustly been put to death, was restored by her to life under the name of Virbius.

219 Adonis, or Thammuz, was restored to life by Proserpine, on condition of his spending half the year with her and half with Venus. His annual death and revival are an allegory of winter and summer.

[220] Pirithous, having attempted to carry off Proserpine, was punished by being bound to the wheel of his father, Ixion. He was, however, according to one legend, subsequently released by Hercules.

[221] Women who died suddenly were said to be slain by the arrows of Diana.

[222] The walls of Thebes, "the seven-gated," (to distinguish it from the Egyptian Thebes of the hundred gates,) were raised by the music of Amphion.

[223] Ate is the Goddess of Retribution.

[224] Crissæus Sinus, the Bay of Crissa, the land *devoted* on account of the sacrilege of the Phocians in the Sacred War. This was ended sixteen years after the death of Epaminondas; and the song is imagined to have been composed during the decline of Thebes, between that time and the capture of the city by Philopœmen.

[225] Œdipus, having been exposed as a child, unwittingly killed his father Laius and married his mother Jocasta. He was driven from the throne of Thebes and went into exile, blind, and attended only by his devoted daughter Antigone. Meanwhile a war for the succession raged between his sons, Eteocles and Polynices. The latter brought seven chiefs to his aid, all but one of whom fell before the city. Both princes were killed, and Creon, who became king, forbade their burial on pain of death. This, however, did not deter Antigone from performing the funeral rites.

[226] Pelopidas and Epaminondas delivered Thebes from the Spartan garrison, and destroyed the supremacy which Sparta had exercised over Greece since the time of the Peloponnesian war.

[227] The dragon showed that he was one of the Sparti or sown men, who traced their descent from the dragon's teeth.

[228] The Apian land is the Peloponnesus, so called from Apis, King of Argos.

[229] Sparta boasted that she had no walls but the shields of her sons. The story is well known of the Arcadian contending with the Spartan: "Many of your nation lie on the plains of Mantinea;" and of the Spartan's reply, "But none of your nation lie on the plains of Sparta."

230 Messene was subdued by Sparta after four terrible wars. It revolted with the assistance of Thebes.

231 The Cyparissian Bay was on the west coast of the Peloponnesus.

232 Ithome was one of the chief towns of Messene.

233 Ira was a stronghold of Messene, the capture of which, after a siege of eleven years, ended the second Messenian war. It was, according to prophecy, to fall when the fig-tree drank of the Neda.

234 Thebes was the chief city in Greece of the Æolic branch; the rest were Doric or Ionic.

235 Cadmea was the citadel of Thebes.

236 Iacchus, or Bacchus, was born when his mother Semele perished in consequence of her having unwisely, at Juno's instigation, requested Jupiter to visit her in divine splendour.

237 Hercules accomplished the twelve famous labours.

238 Zethus and Amphion are described by Æschylus as "the sons of Jupiter who ride on white horses."

239 When mankind were destroyed in the Deluge, the earth was replenished from the stones flung over their shoulders by Deucalion and Pyrrha, in obedience to the Delphic oracle.

240 The serpent with his tail in his mouth was the Egyptian emblem of eternity.

241 Cadmus was banished from Sidon by his father, until he should find his sister Europa. Giving up the search in despair, he applied to Apollo, the Pythian god, who directed him to follow a heifer, which would lead him to the kingdom destined for him.

242 Ismenus is a river of Bœotia, near Thebes.

243 The Spartian line is the Sparti, or sown men; not the Spartistæ, or Spartans.

244 Hermione was the daughter of Venus.

245 For Semele's history, see note 236.

246 Agave, in a fit of frenzy, killed her son Pentheus, king of Thebes.

247 Ino married Athamas, who, during a paroxysm of madness, killed one of his sons, Learchus, and was about to kill the other, Melicertes; but Ino fled with him across the white plain in Megaris, and threw herself with the boy into the sea.

248 Laius was father of Œdipus. (*See* note 225.)

249 Bacchus extended his conquests to India.

250 Bacchus found Ariadne deserted by Theseus, raised her to heaven and placed her crown among the constellations.

251 Theseus, after being freed by Hercules from his captivity in Hades, attempted to eject Menestheus, who in his absence had seized the throne of Athens. Failing in this, he retired to Scyros, where he was treacherously killed by the king, Lycomedes.

252 Hippolytus, son of Theseus, was unjustly accused by his stepmother, Pyrrha. Theseus believed her, and prayed Neptune to punish him; and in passing near the sea-shore his horses took fright, and he was dashed to pieces.

253 Æthra, the mother of Theseus, was enslaved by Castor and Pollux, in revenge for his having carried off their sister Helen.

254 Pentheus, King of Thebes, opposed the introduction of the worship of Bacchus, and was consequently torn in pieces by his mother Agave, and other Bacchanals.

255 Lycurgus, King of Thrace, persecuted Bacchus and his worship on the mountain of Nyseion. He was punished by madness, during which he killed his own son: and he was soon afterwards torn to pieces by horses.

256 Mount Cithæron, in Bœotia, was a famous resort of the Mænads, or Bacchanals.

257 Thyone is a name of Semele.

258 Ino, to whom Bacchus was entrusted on the death of his mother, Semele.

259 Semele. (*See* note 236.)

260 Hercules, son of Alcmena, was begotten by Jupiter, in the form of her husband. The slaughter of the Nemean lion was one of the most famous exploits of Hercules.

261 The last labour of Hercules was to carry off Cerberus from Tartarus, round which Styx flowed nine times.

262 Pirithous, King of the Lapithæ, in Thessaly, was released by Hercules from the punishment which he was undergoing in consequence of his attempt to carry off Proserpine.

263 The labours of Hercules were imposed on him in consequence of his fated subjection to Eurystheus.

264 The Theban armies were arranged for battle in the phalanx.

265 The Sacred Band were the flower of the youth, bound to die on the field of battle rather than fly from it.

266 *See* Longfellow's "Golden Legend," the Nativity, Part III., where the seven angels bring the gifts of Faith, Hope, Charity, Justice, Prudence, Fortitude, and Temperance.

267 An Eastern legend traces the origin of pearls to raindrops falling into the shells.

268 *See* "The Monks of Bangor's March," by Sir Walter Scott.

THE END.